HISTORY OF THE WORLD

Prehistoric and Ancient Europe

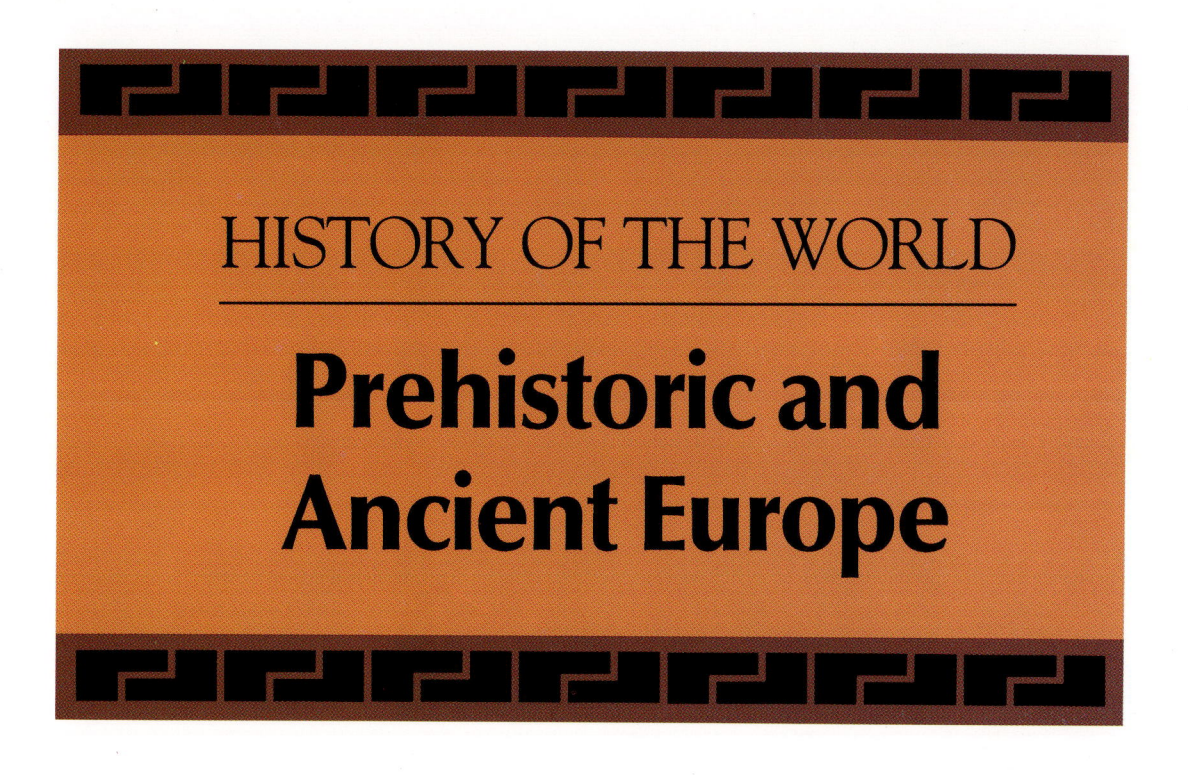

CHERRYTREE BOOKS

A Cherrytree Book

This edition adapted by
A S Publishing

First published by Editoriale Jaca Book s.p.a. Milan
© Editoriale Jaca 1987
First English edition published in United States
by Raintree Publishers
English translation © Raintree Publishers Limited Partnership
Translation by Hess-Inglin Translation Service

This edition first published 1990
by Cherrytree Press Ltd
a subsidiary of
The Chivers Company Ltd
Windsor Bridge Road
Bath, Avon BA2 3AX

Copyright © Cherrytree Press Ltd 1990

British Library Cataloguing in Publication Data
Prehistoric and ancient Europe.
   1. European civilization, ancient period
   I. Williams, Brian II. Series III. Europa preistorica e
antica. *English*
936

   ISBN 0-7451-5104-3

Printed in Hong Kong by Imago Publishing Ltd

All rights reserved. No part of this publication may be reproduced,
stored in a retrieval system, or transmitted, in any form or by any
means without the prior permission in writing of the publisher, nor be
otherwise circulated in any form of binding or cover other than that in
which it is published and without a similar condition including this
condition being imposed on the subsequent publisher

CONTENTS

Europe and Its People	6
Transformation of the European Landscape	8
The First Hunters—Ancient and Middle Paleolithic Periods	11
Development of the Hunters—Recent Paleolithic Period	12
Ancient Artists of Europe	14
The First Mediterranean Farmers	16
Farmers and Hunters Create the First Village	18
Life in Northern Europe and on the Mountains	20
Europeans Discover Metals—The Copper Age	22
The Cultural Revolution Created by Metals	24
The Great Stones—Monuments to the Human Community	26
Bronze Arrives in Europe	29
Life in the Bronze Age	30
Professional Travellers	32
The Origin of European People	34
The Golden Age of Crete	36
The Bronze Age—Civilization of the Greek Mainland	38
The "Dark Centuries" of Greece	40
In the "Dark Centuries," Poems Told of a Heroic Age	42
The Iberians	44
The Italics	46
The Etruscans—Political Structure and Social Life	48
The Etruscans—Merchants, Artisans, Great Artists, and Religious People	50
The Birth of Rome and the Decline of the Etruscans	52
The Iron Age Begins	54
The Warriors of Hallstatt	56
A Refined but Warlike World	58
The Scythians	60
The Celts	62
Europe of the Celts—The Civilization of La Tène	64
Wars and Conquests of the Celts	66
Religion of the Celts	68
Glossary	73
Index	77

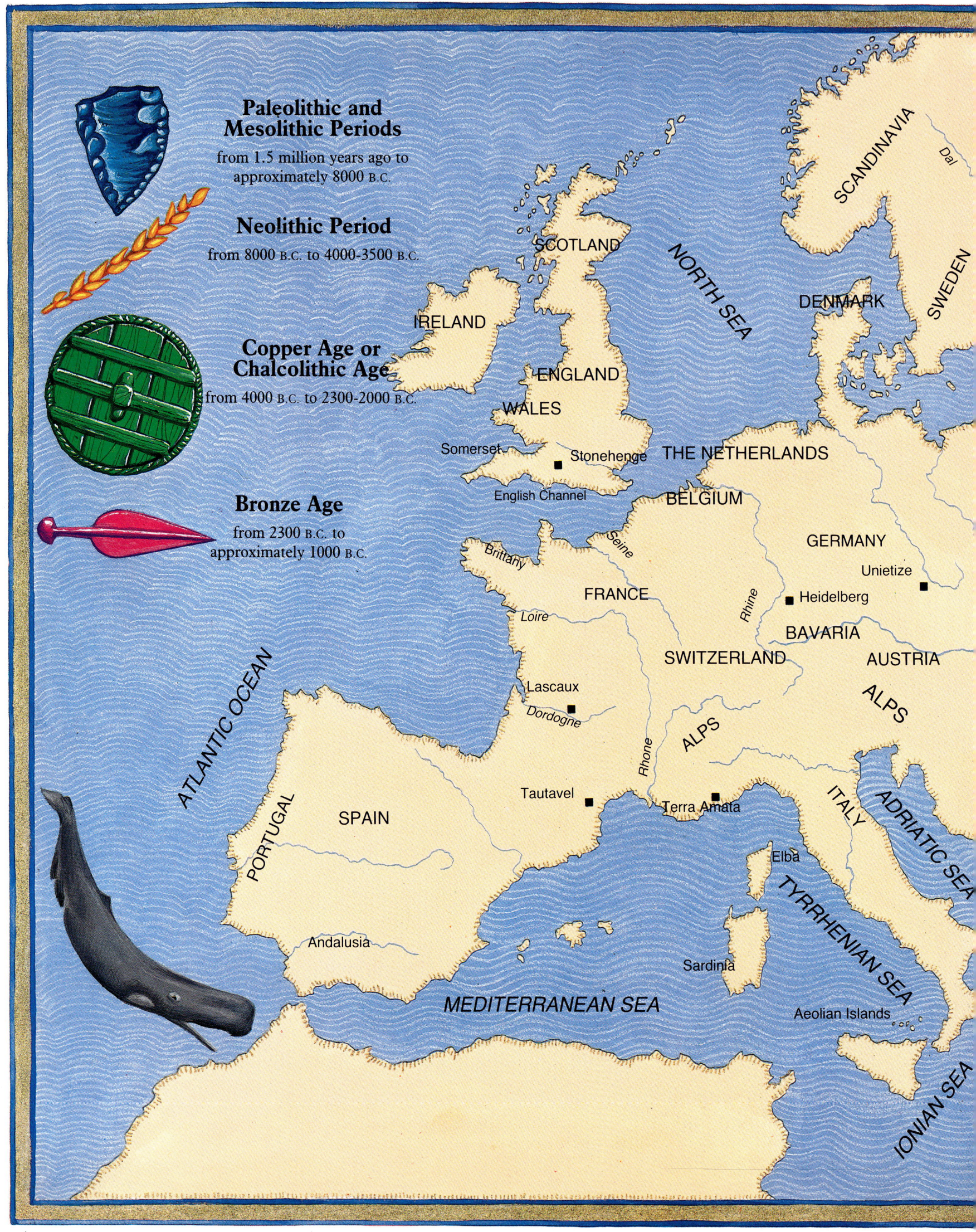

Paleolithic and Mesolithic Periods
from 1.5 million years ago to approximately 8000 B.C.

Neolithic Period
from 8000 B.C. to 4000-3500 B.C.

Copper Age or Chalcolithic Age
from 4000 B.C. to 2300-2000 B.C.

Bronze Age
from 2300 B.C. to approximately 1000 B.C.

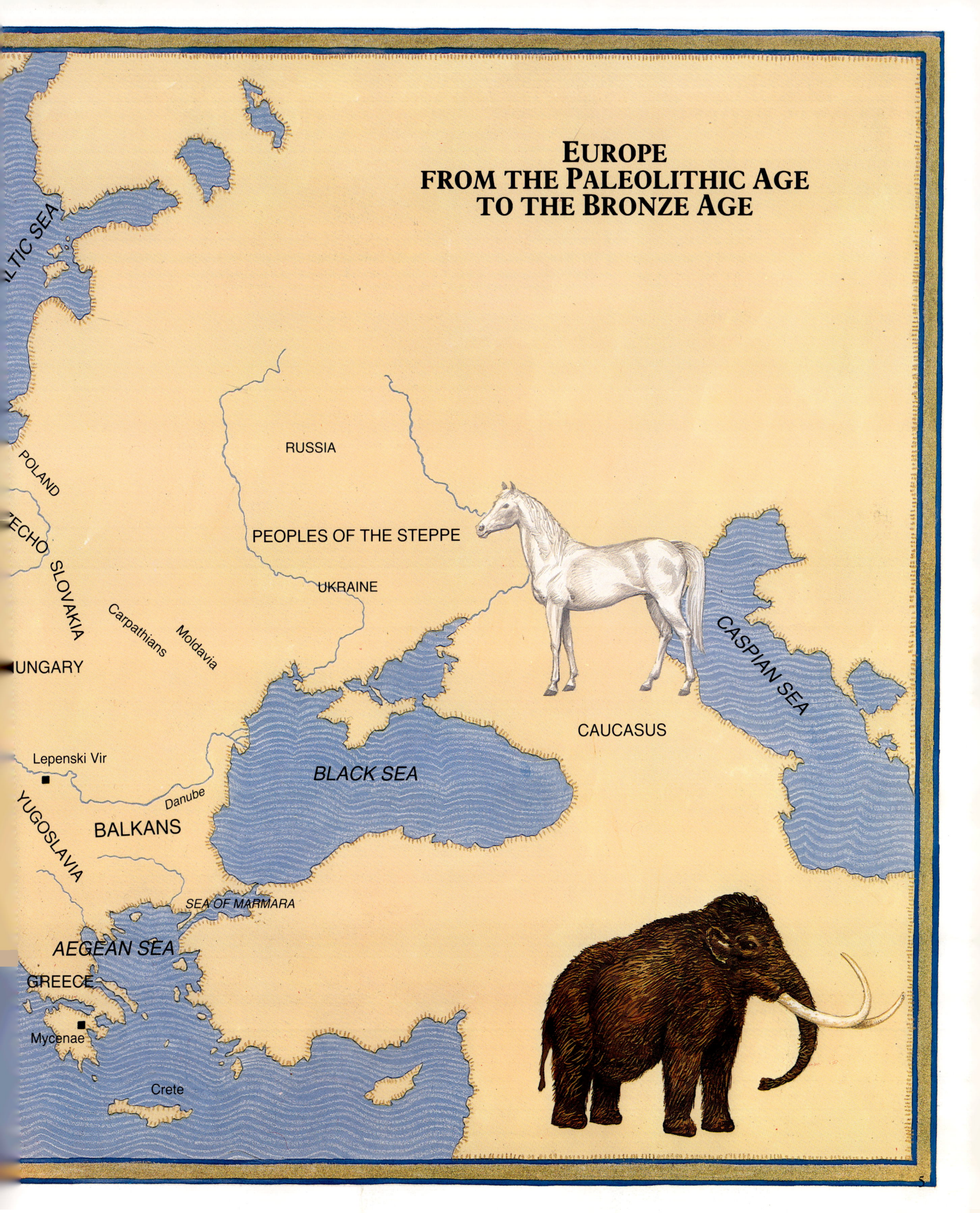

EUROPE FROM THE PALEOLITHIC AGE TO THE BRONZE AGE

BALTIC SEA

POLAND

CZECHOSLOVAKIA

HUNGARY

Carpathians

Moldavia

RUSSIA

PEOPLES OF THE STEPPE

UKRAINE

CASPIAN SEA

CAUCASUS

Lepenski Vir

Danube

BALKANS

BLACK SEA

YUGOSLAVIA

SEA OF MARMARA

AEGEAN SEA

GREECE

Mycenae

Crete

EUROPE AND ITS PEOPLE

Europe—A Regional Mosaic

Europe is the westernmost peninsula of the Asian continent. It is located between a temperate, northern ocean and a warm internal sea. Europe has a great variety of habitats and a highly indented coastline. The European territory is a mosaic of regional habitats, which form a broad succession of climatic zones from the Arctic north to the Mediterranean south. This sequence of climates is concentrated within less than 4,000 kilometres (km) from Norway to the island of Crete.

Ocean and Continents

Europe is washed by the Atlantic Ocean on its western edge. The Mediterranean Sea stretches along its southern boundary. This sea is divided into a series of sections, large and small—the Tyrrhenian, the Adriatic, the Aegean, and the Black seas. Europe is one of the most maritime regions in the world. The ocean moderates climate, so extremes of hot and cold, like those in Asia, do not occur. Europe borders Asia for 2,500 km. The extreme continental climate of central Asia creates dry grasslands which extend as far west as Russia.

Mountains and Plains

The peculiar shape of Europe has yet another set of features. High mountain ranges rise over most of its southern territories, while vast plains cover the eastern and northern regions. The north European plain, which starts in Russia and gradually narrows as it reaches Atlantic France, is geologically more recent than the isolated chain of the Scandinavian mountains to the north. But it is more ancient than the mountain ranges which dominate the south. The heart and the symbol of these mountains are the Alps, white with glaciers. Here is western Europe's highest mountain—Mont Blanc at 4,807 metres high. Further east are the Caucasus, and Europe's highest mountain, Elbruz (5,633 metres). With the exception of the Carpathians, all of the southern European mountains rise close to the coast.

A Land Changed by People

Europe is a region of contrasts. It has always been a fertile area. In the course of creating successive civilizations, people have greatly changed the European landscape.

Europe is dwarfed by Asia.

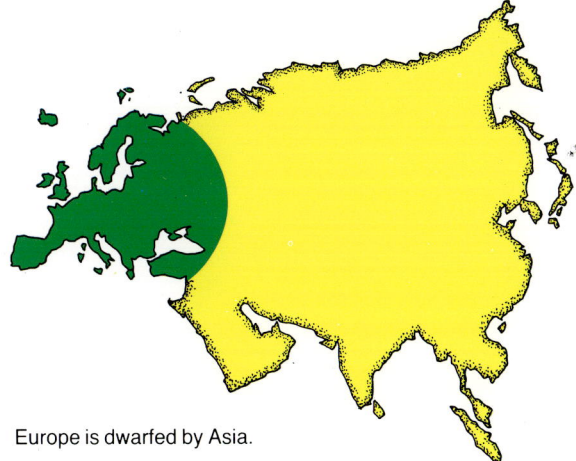

Left: Illustrations show the intermingling of habitats and climates of Europe.

The Habitats of Europe

Vegetation is a convenient way of identifying the different European habitats. The whole of Europe can be divided into three zones in its latitudinal direction—a northern zone with stretches of Arctic territories, a cool temperate zone with a well-marked band of high mountain ranges along its southern edge, and a Mediterranean zone. Combining the various geographical elements mentioned above, the following types of habitats can be distinguished:

1. arctic tundra

2. northern forest, which to the east takes on characteristics of the Russian taiga

3. temperate woodland with deciduous trees mixed with conifers, typical of the continental and Atlantic plains and of the British Isles

4. continental grassland, steppe, and eastern semi-desert in two different forms: a. steppe grassland; b. high mountains within the steppe areas, such as the Caucasian range

5. temperate moors and sandy or uncultivated coastal areas

6. Mediterranean woodland

7. a. Mediterranean scrub; b. Mediterranean grassland, occasionally stretching over wet coastal plains (for example, in Greece). The mountainous regions exhibit zoning by altitude, which has similar features to the latitudinal zoning.

8. mountain forest

9. mountain moors and alpine desert vegetation

Map legend:
1. tundra
2. forest or taiga
3. deciduous and conifer trees
4. a. grasslands, steppes; b. mountainous areas
5. temperate moors, uncultivated coast
6. Mediterranean woodland
7. a. Mediterranean bush; b. wet grasslands
8. mountain forest
9. alpine desert vegetation

7

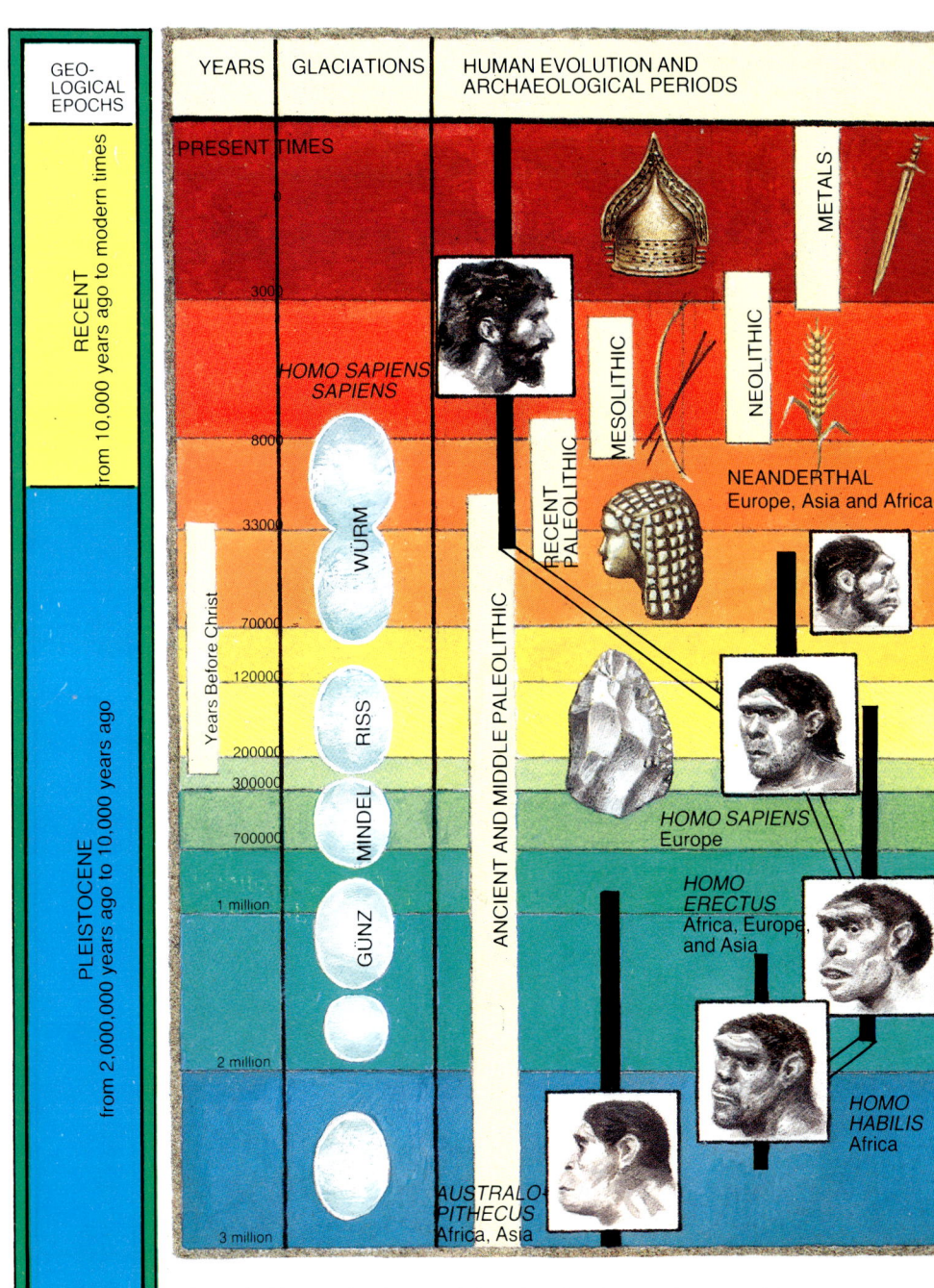

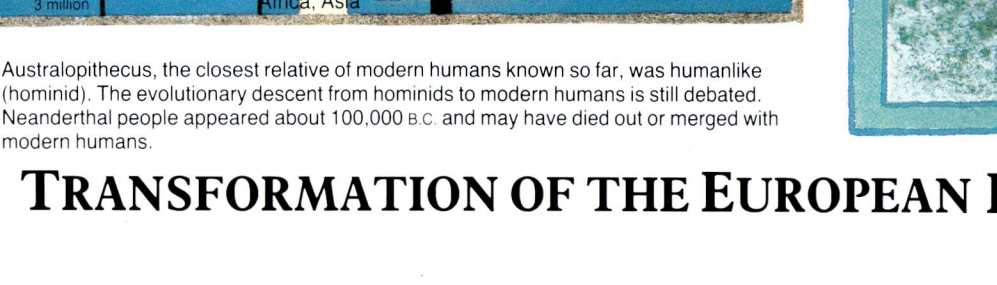

Australopithecus, the closest relative of modern humans known so far, was humanlike (hominid). The evolutionary descent from hominids to modern humans is still debated. Neanderthal people appeared about 100,000 B.C. and may have died out or merged with modern humans.

TRANSFORMATION OF THE EUROPEAN LANDSCAPE

The Earth is Continually Changing

Geographical maps must not give us the impression that present-day landmasses have always existed. Today it is known that continents and oceans have changed greatly, even during the last three or four million years when people have inhabited the earth.

In 1830, Charles Lyell, the founder of modern geology, convinced scholars that coastlines, rivers, and even mountains have changed in the course of time and that they are still in the process of changing. Thirty years later, scientists suggested that the cycles of change were numerous. Charles Darwin proved that these constant changes had greatly affected plants and animals.

In order to understand these patterns of change, it is necessary to think in terms of sufficiently lengthy periods of time. The movement of a centimetre per year will cause a shift of a kilometre in 100,000 years, even without the occurrence of catastrophic events. Many European coasts are moving at this rate today.

The Pleistocene Period

A drastic climatic swing followed by changes in the earth's landscape occurred within the last two million years. The causes of this event are not completely clear but were probably of cosmic origin.

Europe and America were greatly affected by it. At one time, extensive ice caps existed over Scandinavia and Canada and stretched south all the way to the heart of Europe and North America. The ice cap which covers Greenland today is the last trace of the ancient glaciers.

Glaciations Alternated, and the Landscape Changed

The glacial periods were interrupted by warmer times called temperate periods or interglaciations. The coming and going of the glaciers smoothed Northern Europe and about half of the Russian territory. But it also left an indelible mark on central Europe and on the populations which inhabited those regions

The glaciations caused deep changes in the European landscape. When the glaciers increased in size, the territories of central Europe which were free of ice were reduced to a narrow corridor, allowing communication between eastern and western areas. The level of the oceans decreased, and the surface of dry land increased, creating land bridges between areas that were previously separated by water.

An example of the landscape in southern Germany during the Würm glaciation, around 60,000 B.C. The sky is clear, and grass covers the terrain, supporting an abundance of animal life.

The Origin of Humanity— From Africa to Europe, The Fundamental Stages of *Homo Habilis* and *Homo Erectus*

Today, scholars believe that humanlike creatures appeared on earth about 2.5 million years ago in eastern Africa in the great dry savannas which currently form part of the territories of Kenya, Ethiopia, and Tanzania. The first people were around 120 centimetres (cm) tall, and their brains were smaller than those of today's humans. They were called *Homo habilis* because of their skill in making tools. Beside fossils of *Homo habilis*, archaeologists found stone slivers, rudimentary scrapers, and pebbles which were sharpened on stones.

Homo habilis no longer fed merely upon fruit and vegetable matter. They began to eat meat and lived in temporary camp-sites, where groups of people would gather for several days or several weeks. Scholars agree that these early people already had intellectual and artistic capabilities, were able to communicate through language, and had a sense of sociability and perhaps religion. *Homo habilis* gradually spread throughout the African continent, even though its numbers were very low.

Around 1.5 million years ago, another human species called *Homo erectus* appeared in Africa. This species was 140 to 160 cm tall, with a brain larger than that of *Homo habilis*. These African people, whose bone structure is indistinguishable from modern humans, spread to other continents. Fossil remains of this species have been found in Southeast Asia, the Middle East, India, and Europe. *Homo erectus*, who lived from 1.5 million to 70,000 years ago, took some major steps along the path of development. This species developed new hunting techniques, created the first truly organized camp-sites, gained control of the use of fire, developed an aesthetic sense, and understood the concept of symmetry. These people also developed more refined working techniques for wood and stone and created various religious rituals.

during the ancient Stone Age.

When the Scandinavian ice cap and the glaciers in the Alps and in the Carpathians were at their maximum, the territories of central Europe were reduced to a narrow corridor. The land turned into a polar desert. It was parched and devoid of trees and swept by arctic winds which deposited thick layers of debris on the terrain. But the people who had to endure the glaciations in Europe should not be thought of as experiencing conditions similar to those experienced by Eskimos in our own time. Southern Germany and the Po Valley were not like Alaska. Due to their low latitude, they enjoyed sun that was high in the sky, and they had clear skies most of the time.

The Atlantic and Mediterranean regions were covered by woods that had plentiful and varied game. When the glaciers retreated, the climate was even warmer and more humid than it is today. The land was covered by forests of deciduous trees, the soil was fertile, and bands of Paleolithic hunters roamed the region. The expanse of tundra, steppe grassland, and woods varied according to the climatic variations.

Our Epoch

About ten thousand years ago, an interglacial period, which is called the Holocene or Recent Age, began. Who knows if and when the ice will return?

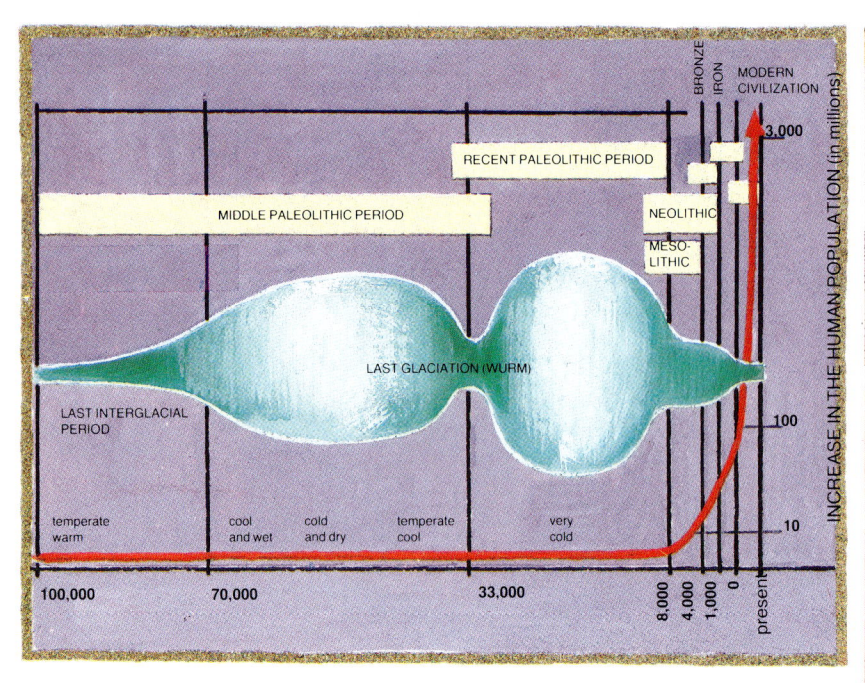

The time chart correlates the most recent climatic changes to the various archaeological epochs. The red line indicates the approximate development of population growth.

Humans learned how to adapt natural rock shelters with structures made of branches and other materials, in order to make them more comfortable as dwelling places.

The Archaeological Periods of Prehistory

The term *Paleolithic*, or Old Stone Age, came into use in 1865 in order to distinguish the "age of the sharpened pebbles" from the term *Neolithic* or New Stone Age, "the age of smooth pebbles". Paleolithic refers to the first great archaeological period in the history of humankind. Archaeology is the science which studies the remains of human activities—objects, tools, buildings, and works of art. Today, the Paleolithic period is divided as follows:

1. Ancient Paleolithic period until around 120,000 B.C.
2. Middle Paleolithic period until around 40,000 B.C., and in Europe until 35,000 B.C.
3. Recent Paleolithic period in Europe from 35,000 B.C. to around 8000 B.C.

At the beginning of the Paleolithic period, humans lived exclusively on vegetation. Later, hunting and fishing were practised.

This meant that humans had to move constantly, and they did not build stable dwellings. In some areas, the shift from the Paleolithic to the Neolithic period is marked by an intermediate period called the Mesolithic period. In the Mesolithic period around 10,000 B.C., humans did not develop new techniques but started to live in a semi-nomadic way. They settled down where there was a plentiful supply of natural resources and ate various species of wild grains. Humans also began to exploit animal herds intensively, developing the first forms of livestock-raising.

The Neolithic period began in the Middle East around eight thousand years ago and later spread to Europe. In this period, humans lived in permanent dwellings and actual villages. The abandonment of nomadism was made possible by the discovery of agriculture. Farming techniques gradually became more and more specialized. Although still practising hunting and fishing with increasingly elaborate techniques, humans also started to domesticate animals like dogs and sheep.

Illustrated is a chip that was detached from a rock with a blow. To the left is the inner side of the chip, in the middle is the outer side, and to the right is the cross section. This chipped pebble was a primitive tool and was grasped at its thickest part as shown in the cross section.

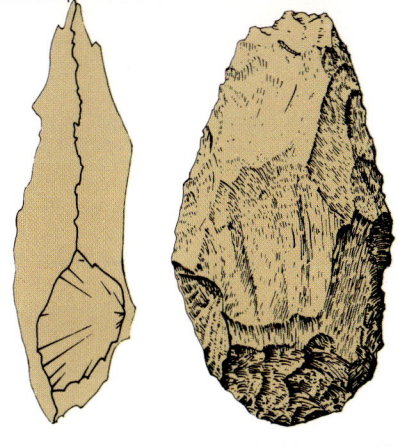

A stone bifacial hand axe, 130,000 years old, found in Le Lazaret in France.

THE FIRST HUNTERS
Ancient and Middle Paleolithic Periods

Humans Arrive in Europe

Homo erectus reached Europe around 1.5 million years ago. Until 700,000 B.C., they lived in the open or in caves, close to fresh water sources, in slightly upland locations. At this time, humans still did not know how to use fire. Before an excavation in Andalusia (Spain) in 1983, no human remains had been found from this period in Europe.

From 700,000 to 400,000 B.C.

Starting from 700,000 B.C., humans began to chip pebbles on two sides in a symmetrical pattern. This was a major step forward both technically and aesthetically. During the interglacial periods, the human populations began to push from the temperate areas into northern Europe, reaching Britain, Belgium, Germany, and Czechoslovakia.

Very little is known about humans in Europe during this period. The first clue was a human jaw found close to Heidelberg in Germany in 1906. More recently, in 1967, excavations in a cave near Tautavel in France have brought to light important human remains dating back to 450,000 B.C.

These early people developed techniques for hunting large carnivores. The meat was used as food, and the skins were used for clothing. Among the animals hunted on the plateaus were musk-oxen, reindeer, and wolves. Mouflons and chamois were hunted on the mountain slopes; while horses, bison, aurochs (wild cattle), rhinoceroses, and elephants were the favourite prey on the plains.

From Fire to Organized Societies

Around 400,000 years ago, humans discovered fire. In Terra Amata, close to Nice in France, several remains of firepits were found. They were built in a temporary campsite which was probably established 380,000 years ago. After the discovery of fire, social activities rapidly developed, and the campsites were better organized. More time was spent in community life and in conversation, thus strengthening the tribal and family bonds.

Around 200,000 years ago when another major glaciation took place, the inhabitants of Europe already knew how to use fire. They hunted in bands composed of several families, hardening the points of their wooden lances with fire. They settled for long periods of time near fresh water, and they made their caves more hospitable by remodelling them with stones and other, lighter materials. They roamed their territories, following the seasonal cycles and the animal migrations, reaching the northernmost regions.

Around 128,000 years ago, the Riss glaciation abruptly ended. At that time, the human populations had already explored all of the European environments except for the arctic regions and had successfully endured the glaciation period, even in very cold areas. They were gradually becoming very efficient hunters. The strength of people was not only in their highly developed manual skills but also in their tendency to develop organized societies. These societies were regulated by discipline in the sharing of food. There were also advances culturally because the young learned the accumulated wisdom of the group through spoken language.

A group of early hunters ambushes an elephant herd.

A winter campground established by a group of hunters on the plains of eastern Europe. The hunter to the left is using a throwing stick. In the centre an animal skin has been stretched in order to be scraped and cleaned, while a woman is making holes in another pelt before sewing it.

Some of the animals that lived in Europe at the time of the glaciations (Pleistocene).

DEVELOPMENT OF THE HUNTERS
Recent Paleolithic Period

Modifications in Techniques

Between 40,000 and 30,000 years ago, major changes occurred in Europe. The hunters began to shape the natural environment around them.

From their ability to split stones into thin slivers, this period has been called Leptolithic (from the Greek meaning "thin stone"). New ways of organizing hunting developed, while the hunters learned how to use bones in addition to stones for the production of elaborate tools. About 27,000 years ago, the first lance points furnished with hook-like barbs, similar to arrowheads, appeared in France. Four thousand years later, thin and sharp slivers began to be widespread, proving that humans were using tools composed of several parts and different materials. A little later, arrowheads with barbs reappeared. Later on, several types of barbs or tips became common on tools made of stone and bone. During the Leptolithic period, the use of "thrown" weapons became widespread. A device called a throwing stick was used to lengthen the throw and the power of penetration of hunting lances. This instrument was undoubtedly used 17,000 years ago and prompted the creation of increasingly lethal lances. These spears were made with bone harpoon-heads or had composite points, formed by the insertion of tiny flint heads on the shafts. Eventually, knowledge of the bow reached Europe and completed this time of rapid progress in toolmaking.

The presence of such a great number of new devices might lead one to think that new populations had come to settle in these regions. However, the possibility of mass migrations is very unlikely. The Leptolithic populations were probably highly receptive to innovations from the outside, but these innovations were all based in Europe.

Southerners and Northerners

In this epoch, two great branches of civilization differentiated within Europe. One was essentially southern, Mediterranean, while the other was based on the vast north European plains.

In the southern regions, from Iberia to the Danube, humans became highly skilled in the use of bone and produced large blades with extended and gradually slanted cutting edges. They expressed primitive religion based on the principle of maleness and femaleness in nature and created numerous paintings and carvings with animal figures.

The vast plains of the eastern and northern regions were the homeland of the Gravettian populations (named after La Gravette, an archaeological site in Dordogne, France). These groups produced increasingly small, sharp blades, with short and steep cutting edges which they mounted on handles and used as knives or lance points. They also produced female statuettes to celebrate special occasions. Elsewhere in France, north of the Alps and the Balkans, the two civilizations were largely contemporary and occasionally intermingled.

From *Homo Erectus* to *Homo Sapiens Sapiens*

The last stage of human development was reached in the course of the last 100,000 years (the period of existence of *Homo sapiens* on earth), and in particular in the period starting 40,000 years ago (when *Homo sapiens sapiens* developed). At its first appearance, *Homo sapiens sapiens* was already as tall as average humans of today and possessed modern-day brain size. What is most important is that these beings already expressed themselves like modern humans. Their art in the caves was by no means inferior to contemporary paintings. Social life was similar to that of nomadic people of modern times. Their form of dwelling, a transportable hut, would remain unchanged for thousands of years.

Some important technical innovations of the recent Paleolithic period included reindeer antler harpoons, a stone point mounted on a shaft, and the bow.

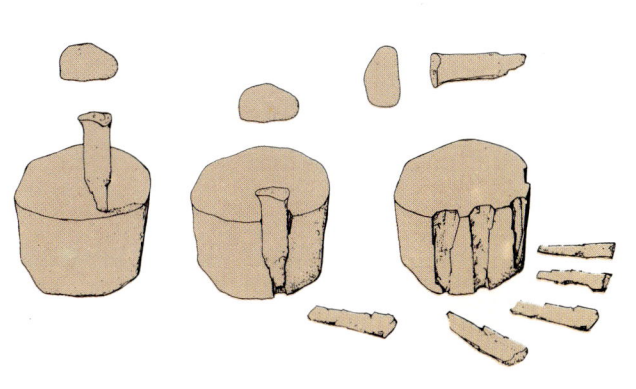

Thin blades were split from a block of flint.

ANCIENT ARTISTS OF EUROPE

Energy and Tools

From the northern regions to the Mediterranean, the mastery of fire in domestic life was of great importance. Different kinds of firepits were built and every kind of combustible material was tried including crumbled bones and coal (in Moravia and in Switzerland). The habit of boiling food in hide containers became common. Boiling altered the characteristics of the food, causing a revolution in body metabolism and even affecting the growth of human beings.

Little is known about the kind of clothing worn and the tools used in daily activities, but there is enough evidence to suggest that the European populations wore clothes made of animal hides which were carefully tailored and sewn, and sometimes even buttoned with small bone discs. Eyed needles were used, and the tendons of the legs of herbivores were turned into thread. The people who lived in windy and cold climates or who roamed the mountains wore trousers, hooded jackets, and certainly also footwear for every kind of terrain. Body paintings as well as ornaments and perhaps tattoos were believed to help protect the body.

The Birth of Great Art

The populations living during the last Paleolithic period in Europe, from around 35,000 to 8000 B.C., looked like modern humans. Apart from the language and technical skills of these people, the best testimony to their intellectual and cultural level is their art, visible today inside caves and under rock shelters. Artistic objects that have been found are made of various materials such as stone, bone, ivory, and reindeer antler.

In regard to the numerous groups of painted figures, it seems clear that prehistoric artists were trying to get across a message which often referred to human fertility and hunting. Whatever their meaning, the abundance of painted figures on the walls of caves has provided information on animal species and on the natural and cultural environment of Paleolithic humans. There are huge surfaces of painted rock in France and Spain. This might mean that the entire community was involved in the artistic project.

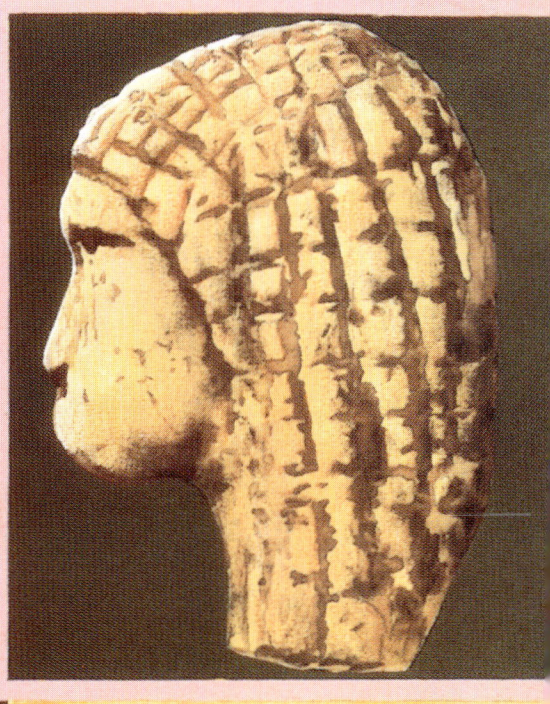

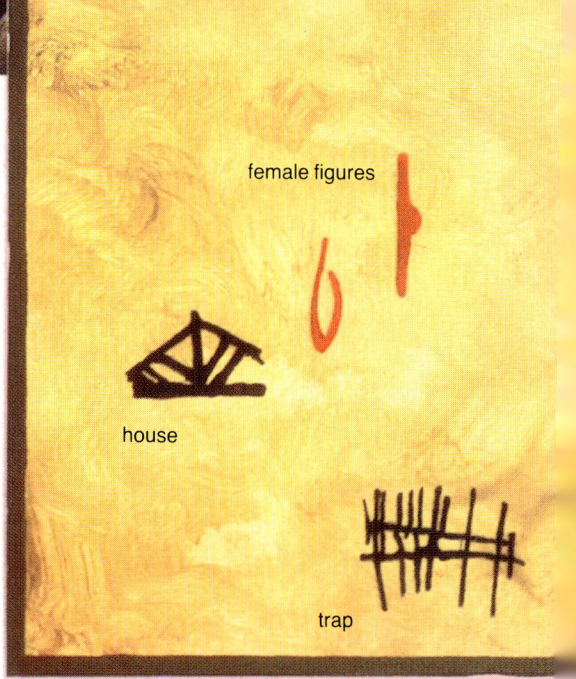

In the same sites as the paintings, remains of large tree trunks are sometimes found. Perhaps these trees were felled and transported to the site to be used for the building of scaffolding, and this was certainly not the work of a single individual. Besides these, hundreds of stone lamps (which were probably filled with animal fat and used to illuminate dark caves) have been found.

Painted caves were temples of a sort, expressing religious beliefs. This means that human beings were striving to establish a relationship with some sort of deity which would enable them to face the events of their lives as well as their questions about death in a more secure fashion. Proof of the sacredness of these paintings and carvings rests in the fact that at different times, sometimes at intervals of hundreds of years, prehistoric artists returned to paint where works already existed. They would even paint on the same slab of rock, overlaying new paintings and carvings on top of existing ones. They did not act from purely artistic inspiration, especially considering that other similar and unused rock slabs were available close by. For these prehistoric artists, it was important to work where others had already painted and carved rocks.

Most of the figures left on rock walls by the prehistoric artists depict animals. Horses are the most commonly represented, but there are also bison, wild oxen, bear, antelope, wild cats, rhinoceroses, and more rarely fish, frogs, and grasshoppers. Human figures are not very common in the art of the caves and in the decoration of objects. When they appear, they often have peculiar deformations. Human faces resemble animal faces, or human limbs have animal features. For example, an owl's head may be combined with a horse's tail and a reindeer's antlers. These oddities have led to the belief that the images depicted were of a masked sorcerer on the occasion of some important ceremony. Often geometric figures appear beside the animal patterns.

The art of the caves is exceptional. The figures have remained at the site where they were painted and are often very well preserved. Finding these great works of art in caves was fortunate. Artists probably also painted on bark, hides and wood, but none of these works has been preserved to modern times.

Death as a Passage Into Another Life

During the long period in which artistic expression first blossomed, numerous burial sites were used by the peoples of Europe. Many objects which accompanied the dead in their tombs have been perfectly preserved. In particular, typical of this period are ornaments made of shells and pierced deer teeth. The ancient peoples wanted to demonstrate their affection for the dead, and they wanted to give the dead a means for survival in another life. They surrounded the bodies with food, weapons, and tools.

Red ochre was frequently used in the burial procedures. This is a natural dye extensively used for painting and to dye hides and weapons. It was also spread over the bodies of the dead, as shown by traces which have been found on skeletons. One explanation for the use of ochre is that it symbolized blood, the essential element of life.

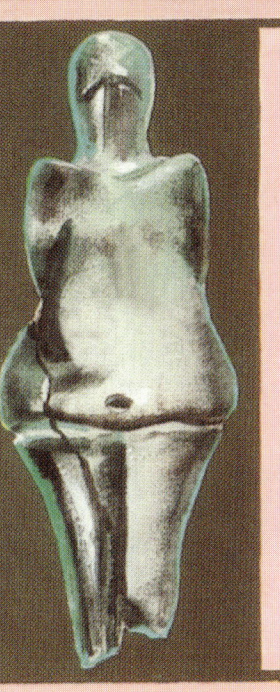

Above: A burial ceremony, where red ochre was sprinkled over the body.
Opposite page: A hunting scene is depicted. The prey was feared and respected at the same time.
Right: Ancient artists paint a ritual painting on a rock.
Centre left: A woman's head made from ivory from Brassempouy, France, 30,000 years old.
Centre right: A clay figurine of a woman, of the same age, Czechoslovakia.

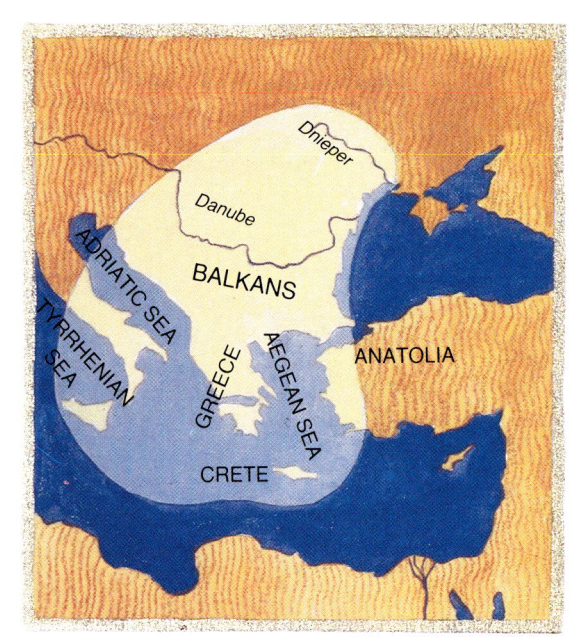

The region of Europe where the first forms of agriculture developed.

Left: Some examples of wheat. The first four species from the top left corner are wild; the others are cultivated.
Above is a farming village in Moldavia. The larger building at its centre was used as a place of worship. This was the first European temple, dating back to 6000 B.C.

THE FIRST MEDITERRANEAN FARMERS

Domestication of Animals

Around 8000 B.C., the Mesolithic tribes who lived around the Tyrrhenian, Aegean, and Black seas were extremely receptive to the idea of domestication. They realized that animals could be raised, not just hunted. During the glaciation period, there was a close interdependence between some hunters and the herds of reindeer. Along the coasts of the Mediterranean and the Middle East, the same kind of dependence had developed between humans and gazelles. It was also discovered that by putting the seeds of nutritious plants in the soil, it was possible to cultivate them. Annual wild grains bearing large seeds on frail ears were grown and were the forerunners of today's cultivated varieties. The knowledge of growing plants and raising animals permitted the collection of larger quantities of food closer to inhabited areas. People lived in huts made of compacted clay applied to a frame of poles and branches, and later of unfired mud bricks.

The Religion of Ancient Europe

Areas around the Mediterranean Sea and in the steppes which stretch between the Adriatic Sea and the Dnieper River are sometimes known as ancient Europe. Between the seventh and the fourth millennia, this intensely creative area, the axis of which was the Danube, witnessed the blossoming of a unified culture. A unity of religious concepts and ritual activities developed.

Life was considered sacred because it originated from a divinity. This concept was rendered in numerous symbols: a cosmic egg from which all living creatures originated, water, the snake, and other animals. The image of woman represented fertility, allowing for the human race to perpetuate itself. The earth, or Great Mother, gave people sustenance. Therefore, the woman became the very image of life itself. Thousands of statuettes were produced, portraying the female deity. People were part of the great rhythm of the cosmos, which is born, dies, and is born again.

The village became the centre of religious experience, a sacred place where prayers and rituals were performed. Altars and temples were raised in the centre of the village and soon the temple became the most important building. Life was centred on what the temple represented, and in a sense contained—the mystery of the bonds between the earthly

Ritual offerings are presented to a priest. The "firing" of clay figurines was an important part of the ceremony.

The altar in the temple contains ritual figurines. Also pictured are the clay throne and a kiln.

A small ritual table.

world and the other world. It was home to the gods and the spirits, where people originated and would return. Gods and spirits could communicate with the earthly world and the other world through special rituals.

The Neolithic Period

Between 10,000 and 8,000 years ago, there was great activity among the gulfs and archipelagoes of the eastern Mediterranean. The various regions were connected by a network of social relationships, in particular by sea traffic.

A new way of life based mainly on the production of food developed by the seventh millennium (or 6000s) B.C. This revolutionary change, a landmark in human history, occurred in many places, including on the Mediterranean coasts. It was similar to what had happened in Anatolia and in the Middle East at slightly earlier times. Among the various features that characterized the new way of life were herbivore raising, grain cultivation, and the invention of ceramic techniques. These factors did not always develop simultaneously. One or the other tended to prevail depending on local conditions. The practice of hunting and gathering was never fully abandoned. With the development of the idea that food could be produced following natural cycles and not just from hunting or gathering in the wild, humans entered the stage called the Neolithic period. They acquired the capability of planning and a confidence that was unknown to the hunting populations.

The First Farming Villages

The first Neolithic populations rapidly spread along the coasts of the Aegean Sea and in the Balkans. Islands such as Crete were colonized in the first centuries of the seventh millennium. The human populations were still living in caves and temporary buildings. However, in areas where the soil was sufficiently fertile and the production techniques were more advanced, both natives and newcomers built small villages with longer lasting, more solid huts.

The early farmers raised sheep and oxen and cultivated two or three species of primitive wheat. The oxen were perhaps the result of the domestication of the European aurochs, a large form of wild cattle (now extinct).

pick axe for use in fields

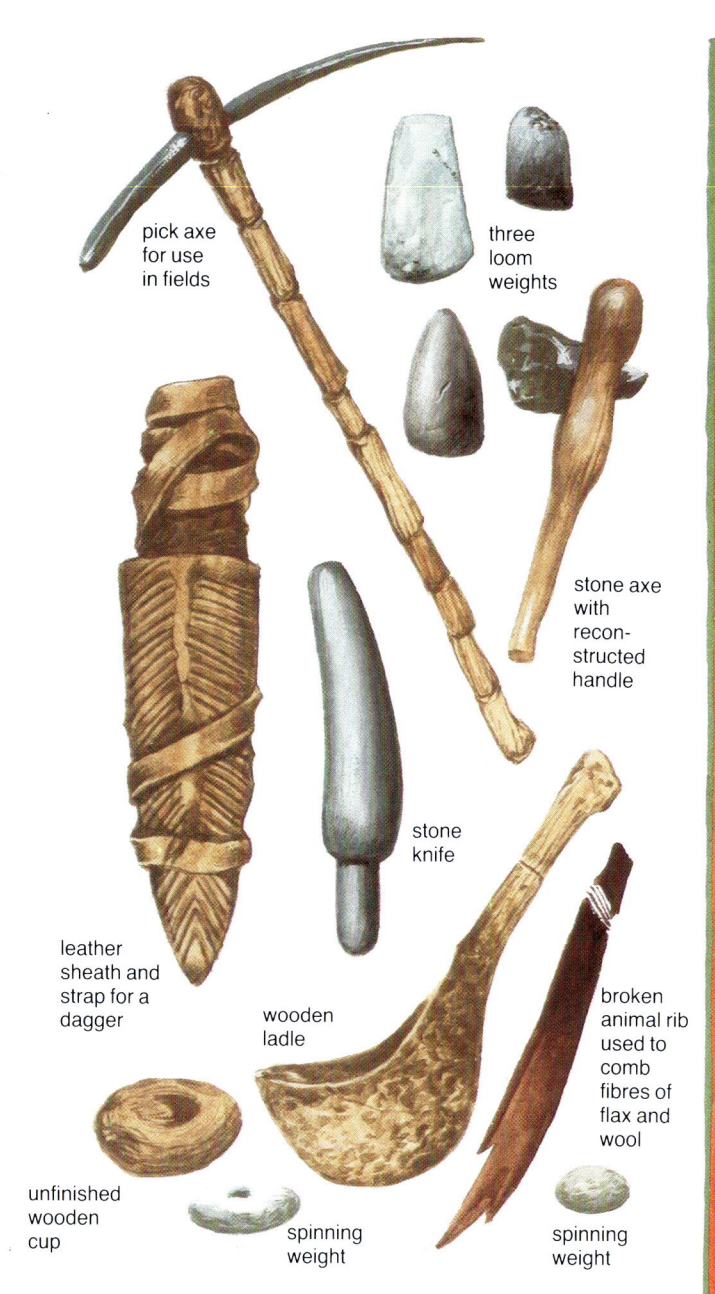

three loom weights

stone axe with reconstructed handle

leather sheath and strap for a dagger

stone knife

wooden ladle

broken animal rib used to comb fibres of flax and wool

unfinished wooden cup

spinning weight

spinning weight

A scene from everyday life in a village of the Neolithic period. The pathways between the houses were built by placing tree logs close to each other over the swampy terrain. Inside a hut, a weaving loom is shown.

FARMERS AND HUNTERS CREATE THE FIRST VILLAGE

Spread of the Neolithic Culture

Europe of long ago was characterized by temperate forests and by harsh winters north of the Mediterranean and the Balkans. It was a vast region with rolling hills covered by woods with dark rich soils. Here, farming life became predominant mostly through the arrival of Neolithic communities from the south and the east.

It started about 5800 B.C. and rapidly developed in the fifth millennium. By 4000 B.C., the first farmers reached the British Isles in northwestern Europe. In the south, where Europe becomes a true mosaic of environments—in the Po Valley and in the Rhone Valley, in Iberia, and in Atlantic France—the new way of life resulted mainly from the absorption of the Mesolithic populations, many of which had already learned how to raise animals.

In the early Neolithic period, two different cultures started to take shape—a mixed farming and animal husbandry culture in southern and southeastern Europe and a nomadic life in western and northern Europe. The border between the two cultures crossed the Alps and the Italian peninsula. Along this border the two cultures confronted each other, thus evolving and maturing. The east and south were primarily farming oriented for a long time, while societies in the west either remained hunters or pastural nomads who lived off domesticated animals.

Livestock Raisers, Farmers, and Hunters

People of the Neolithic period living on the continent showed a close relationship with those living in the areas of the Mediterranean and Black seas. On the continent, the variety of the environments and the different seasons pushed humans to wider adaptations and more

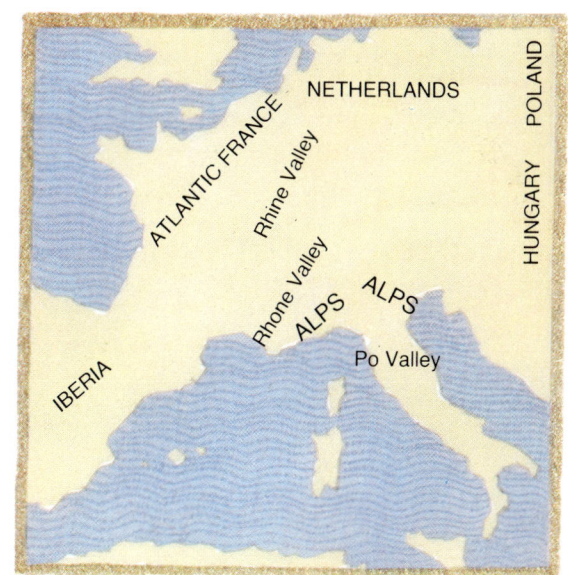

Temperate Europe

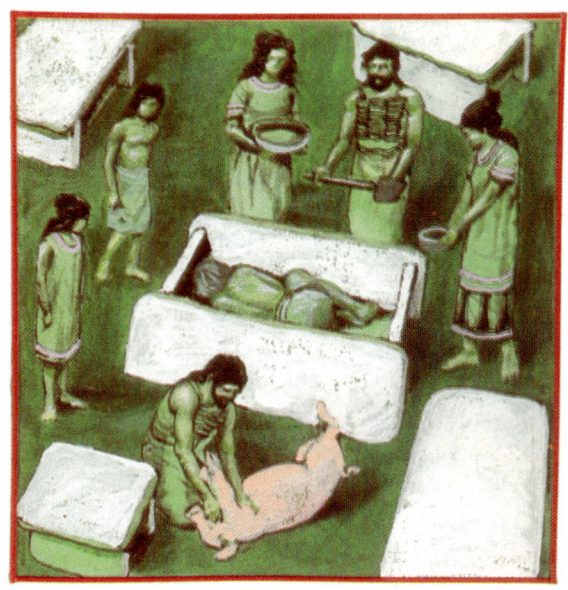

A burial in a stone coffin is supervised by mourners bringing gifts to accompany the dead body.

Changes in Farming Life

The life of a farmer was characterized by the use of new products and new tools. Neolithic people ate wheat, barley, millet, peas, beans, lentils, milk, and fermented beverages. Cooking was based on boiling food. Wool and linen made their entrance into European life. The presence of spindle weights and loom weights is evidence of the invention of weaving in European lands. Ceramics and wood were used to make containers for food, bowls, and pots.

technical inventions than in the southern regions. The use of wood replaced the use of clay because wood was the most abundant natural resource in the temperate habitats. Knowledge of the secrets of wood and of the forests was the basis for the economic success of these colonizers of the Danube and Rhone regions.

The forest environment was characterized by the presence of trees, fresh water, and game. The first Neolithic populations of Europe learned to combine the information about these known resources with new ideas in agriculture, vegetable growing, and animal raising. The true difference, the true revolution of the Neolithic period, was the domestication of plants and animals.

The Birth of the Rural European Village

In the fourth millennium B.C., well into the Neolithic period, people actively explored the areas between rivers and started to colonize land on the hills and in the woods. The pick axe became more refined and was eventually replaced by a tool which was used to break very hard terrain. This tool was a rudimentary plough and was pulled by men or women. In this way, fields were created. Dry land began to be farmed by relying on seasonal rains, and people began to select varieties of wheat, barley, and vegetables which were best suited to the different European habitats. Materials from the woods were carefully chosen and used, and game was still hunted.

The population grew, creating the need for wider spaces, more food, and especially better productive efficiency and new ways of coexistence. In the space of a few generations, true rural villages sprang up throughout temperate Europe as well as in the peninsulas.

A group of people return from a gathering expedition in the Alps. In the foreground are rock carvings from Switzerland.

A religious ritual practised in a Neolithic Alpine society. The posture of the worshippers corresponds to the posture of the figures which are carved on the rock.

LIFE IN NORTHERN EUROPE AND ON THE MOUNTAINS

During the 3000s B.C., well into the Neolithic period, small regional groups of people lived according to a custom that was starting to be widespread and was called "European". This way of life was relatively uniform and required regular communication between distant communities through environments and climates which were widely different. People were already using boats dug from oak trunks. Large and medium-sized continental rivers came alive with traffic. This traffic helped the exchange of goods as well as the movement of people and ideas. Oxen were used to pull ploughs and sleighs, helping to transport people and goods on land.

Fishermen and Shepherds of the Northern Regions

Scandinavia and the lands of northern Europe were colonized by farmers between the fifth and fourth millennia. But besides groups of farmers, there were also tribes of hunters, fishermen, and gatherers continuing to follow ancient customs. Between the fourth and third millennia, tribes of farmers appeared in Sweden, around the Dal River, at the northernmost limit for farming. At about the same time, Neolithic life reached the Atlantic coast. On the coasts of Portugal, Biscay, Brittany, Great Britain, and Scandinavia, communities of fishermen became important. These com-

Left: Villages in England were surrounded by embankments supported by poles. Beyond the villages were cultivated fields. The large construction to the right is the necropolis, or house of the dead.

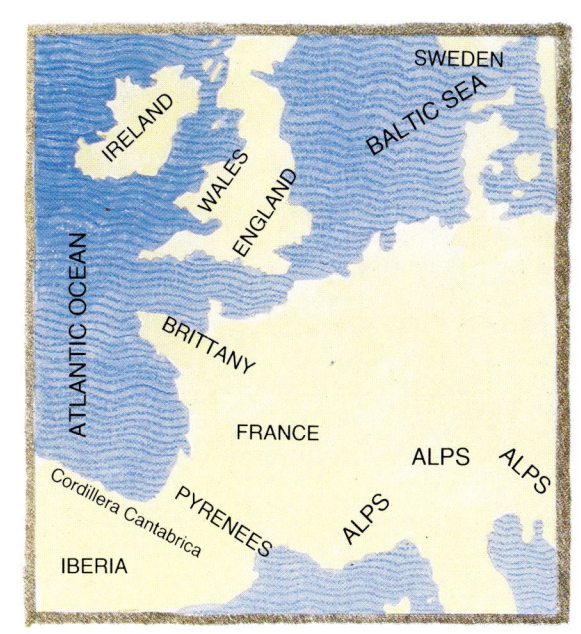

Northern Europe, showing the positions of the Alps and the Pyrenees.

munities were interconnected by a network of trade routes which followed the western seas.

Clearing the Forests

Around 4700 B.C. in Brittany and a little later in the British Isles, all the way to the remote coasts of Ireland, Denmark, and Sweden, the Mesolithic populations learned farming techniques and produced rough clay pots. They also built gigantic longhouses using logs, soil, and stone. The shapes of these houses varied according to the different regions, and they soon became prestigious tombs and centres of ceremony.

In Ireland and England, the local leaders who promoted these changes wanted to be cremated after death. They also adopted the custom of fastening their clothing with large horn pins and began to use molluscs and other animals as offerings.

These people welcomed the idea of settlement in the hills and continually developed new farmland by opening up clearings in the forest with the use of fire (approximately 3800-3200 B.C.). In the grassy moors and rolling hills of England, the villages began to be surrounded by embankments reinforced with poles or by fences. The same kinds of structures were built in southern France and in Portugal.

Pioneer Communities in the Alps

Undoubtedly the Alps, like any other European mountain range, had been roamed by bands of Paleolithic and Mesolithic hunters in previous times. Starting from the fourth millennium, groups of people settled in these areas, even at the highest altitudes and in the most remote regions of the interior. In some cases, in the third millennium, the Alpine settlements became greatly advanced centres of cultural creativity, capable of influencing the surrounding territories.

The Alps and the North

The Alps and the regions of northern Europe had many features in common. When Neolithic people replaced Paleolithic hunters, they had to adapt anew to the mountains. Some European communities realized that, provided they regulated their lives according to natural cycles and wisely saved their energy, the Alps and the northern regions could prove to be very hospitable.

Some animals were chosen as particularly fit to help people in this harsh environment. In the Alps, herders roamed the land with sheep. In Scandinavia, the reindeer was the main animal herded. Summer was the season for gathering a year's supply of wild fruit, mushrooms, medicinal herbs, and other plants.

The development of settlements formed by tight clusters of houses, camouflaged to suit the environment, was typical of these cultures. Dwellings were often built with stones. Social cooperation acquired a new dimension and became a fundamental instrument for survival. The northern and alpine settlers created their own culture, different from that of the inhabitants of the lowlands.

21

EUROPEANS DISCOVER METALS— THE COPPER AGE

A Great Discovery

The first metals, gold and copper, were discovered in various locations in western Asia and in the Balkans region. Between 4500 and 3500 B.C., a complex metal technology developed in the Balkans, then gradually spread to most of Europe by approximately 1500 B.C. It was only after 800 B.C. when the use of iron became widespread in the Mediterranean that the first advanced civilizations appeared in Europe. The rocks which contained copper minerals were an attractive blue-green colour. They contained malachite, copper carbonate.

Humans of the Neolithic period were attracted by these bright rocks, considering them somehow magical. They noticed that the small clusters of malachite could sometimes have peculiar shapes and could be ground into a powder. Perhaps it was noticed by accident that these peculiar stones melted if exposed to fire or heat.

The Mineral Wealth of the Soil

With the advent of metallurgy, Europe discovered a new form of wealth in the soil. From the Danubian plain, the idea of the precious stones spread to the Neolithic populations of central and Alpine Europe. Following the Neolithic trade routes, it reached as far as Sardinia and Andalusia.

In the western regions of the Tyrrhenian Sea, Iberia, and the Atlantic Ocean, the new technology of metals alternated and competed with the traditional technology of stone. Metal objects were constructed as copies of stone objects and vice versa, depending on the material available at different times and on the preferences of different people.

The Wheel

The invention of the wheel also belongs to this time period. The wheel (at first a crude, solid wooden device) was used for the creation of small carts, similar to modern wheelbarrows. The carts were used to transport tools, farm produce, and minerals for short distances. Large wagons caused a revolution in the systems of transport.

In the Tyrolean mountains, copper miners extract the mineral from surface veins. The larger rocks are cracked by sudden changes in temperature – pouring water on heated boulders.

By 2500 B.C., small wheeled wagons were in use.

The Metal Trade

Stone and metal became fundamental items in the long distance trade of rare materials that developed in Europe. The word trade refers to the transfer of goods from one population to another. In the same way, styles and customs were passed between different societies. This was the process by which some cultural innovations were rapidly spread and shared over vast areas of the continent and at opposite ends of seas and mountain ranges.

Towards the Bronze Age

When primitive smelters worked, they noticed that the presence of small quantities of metals other than copper made the copper slightly harder. They tried to identify these different substances and, when possible, to quantify them. The principle of metal alloy had been discovered. A copper mineral with traces of arsenic, found at some sites, was highly prized. This alloy was made by the direct addition of increasingly high quantities of arsenic to the mineral. Humans were beginning to experiment seriously with the chemical and physical properties of metals and produced new, durable substances. The new, harder metal could be employed for the manufacture of functional instruments, not only for ornamental ones. The days when copper had only artistic use was over. Metal acquired new value.

Two-bladed copper axe with wooden handle

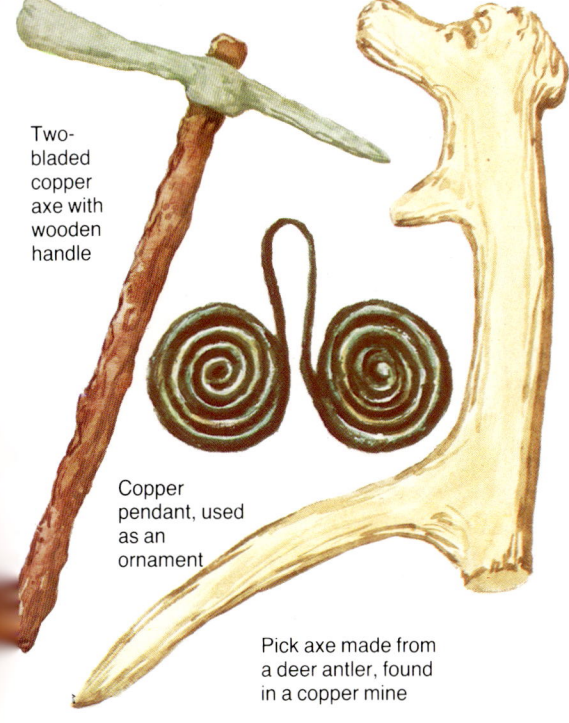

Copper pendant, used as an ornament

Pick axe made from a deer antler, found in a copper mine

The Stone Age is Followed by the Metal Ages
—the Bronze Age, the Copper Age, and the Iron Age

In Europe, the Neolithic period ended in the fourth millennium B.C. The Bronze and Iron ages were characterized by work with gold and copper. The invention of the wheel allowed for a more rapid spread of technical discoveries, as well as of new philosophical concepts. Copper had different properties from stone. Copper is much lighter and more pliable, but it cannot replace all the stone, bone, or wood in the manufacture of tools.

The use of metal to produce weapons, tools, and personal ornaments was attained in the Bronze Age. Bronze was an alloy of copper and tin, and its production required complex processing. This created the development of true artisan activity, the first form of industry. The figure of the blacksmith was held in high esteem in all societies. This period was followed, around the first millennium, by the Iron Age.

During this time, different populations with their own characteristics and ethnic identities began to appear in Europe. Their written language spread greatly. The term *prehistory* refers to civilizations that did not have a written language. Writing was already used by various civilizations during the Bronze Age, but the shift from prehistory to history took place in Europe only during the Iron Age. The Iron Age lasted until two centuries ago, when the Industrial Revolution marked the beginning of modern times.

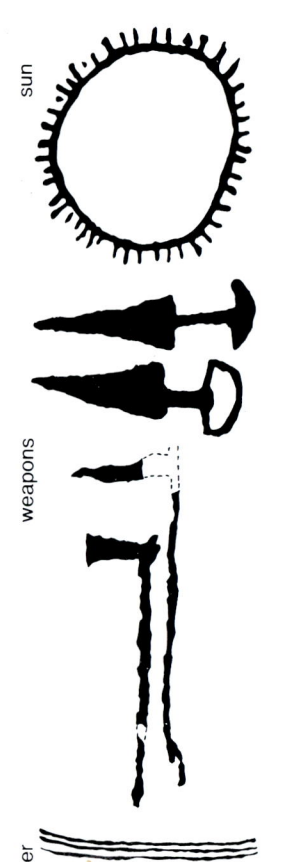

The process of painting a menhir in Val Camonica, Italy. The dyes were obtained by pulverizing various minerals.

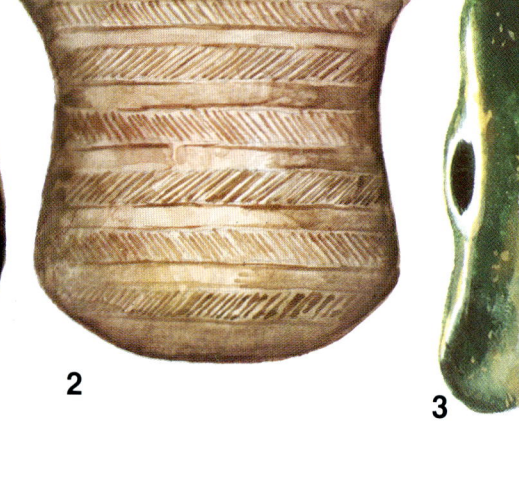

Left: Typical symbols taken from a carved rock. The sun indicates the sky. The knives and the axes are a symbol for the earth. The river is the passageway into the lower world.

1) This clay pot was decorated with rope impressions. It is an example of corded ware from western Switzerland, 2500 B.C. **2)** This vessel is shaped like an inverted bell. On its outer surface, decorated stripes alternate with plain bands. It is an example of bell-shaped ware from Brittany, western France, 2500 B.C. **3)** A double-headed stone axe. It is a typical ceremonial axe used by the same people who made corded ware.

THE CULTURAL REVOLUTION CREATED BY METALS

The Cosmos Painted on Rocks

History was marked in approximately 3200 B.C. by an abrupt change which had an impact on the whole of Europe. Some scholars believe that the basics of modern European culture were laid at that time. The use of metals and the invention of the wheel were at the centre of a major technological revolution. This was evident with the development of a new kind of religion and a new concept of life.

The vision of the universe as held by people during this time was extremely clear as can still be seen today in the rock paintings of this period. The reality of the cosmos was depicted on rocks as being divided into three levels. The upper level represented the sky and was symbolized by the sun—dispenser of light, warmth, and life. The middle level represented the earth, which was the world of human activities and was usually symbolized by daggers or other weapons. The lower level was occupied by a river or a plough furrow, indicating the borderline with the world of the dead.

The various types of rocks were sometimes part of a mountain slope, but usually they were raised on end (menhir) or were carved or cut by humans (stele). Stele were often carved in the shape of human beings, but are not as tall as an adult. Even when they look like people, their meaning is still related to the cosmos. The shape of a sun could resemble a human face. Some stele closely represent human figures because their parts can be identified as faces, arms, jewellery, and weapons. Stele were carved using stone implements and were painted with natural dyes, mostly powdered minerals. Most likely the dyes were applied with sticks with shredded points that functioned like brushes. Many rocks were painted or carved during this period.

The Indo-Europeans

This new wave of ideas and artistic styles moved through the whole continent—Russia, the Caucasus, the Alps, the Mediterranean, and western Europe. The identity of the people and the borders of their territories are not clearly determined mainly because movements of small groups from one region to the next were frequent.

From the end of the Bronze Age, the identity of these populations became increasingly evident. People who had developed a new concept of the cosmos or had come into contact with it were called Indo-Europeans. The name *Indo-European* did not imply that the all the people belonged to the same race, as was once believed. The name referred to people who held the same beliefs about the

A ceremony of rock decoration in Italy.

nature of the universe and who had a similar language. French, German, Italian, Lithuanian, Russian, Hittite, Iranian, and Sanskrit all belong to the same family of languages called the *Indo-European* languages. These populations probably were not from India or Europe, as the word Indo-European seems to suggest. It is more likely that they came from Central Asia.

The Indo-Europeans were livestock herders with a strong sense of family and ancestry and a patriarchal tradition. They seemed to place minor importance on farming. They domesticated the horse and used it for transportation. Socially, they developed a hierarchy with different people having different degrees of power and responsibility. They accepted a universal god who was omnipotent and who was considered the father of the human race. Within the religious beliefs of these people, there was the concept of a god who was superior to all other gods. Subservient to this god were other deities of nature and of the world of the dead. Among them were a goddess of the crops, a god of water in the shape of a snake or bird, and many others.

The Art of Ceramics

Significant evidence of the cultural development and artistic sense of the people living at the beginning of the Bronze Age is found in the beauty of the shapes of their ceramics. Corded ware consisted of rounded vases decorated with a fine-striped pattern created by pressing ropes into wet clay. These ceramic objects, typical of central Europe and Russia, were widespread and were probably the starting point for the development of bell-shaped vessels and cups. Decorated stripes alternate with plain stripes, and the patterns are simple and elegant.

One style was widespread especially along the Rhine, but local styles also developed. The areas where most finds were collected include the coasts of England, Spain, Portugal, France, and the river areas of central Europe.

menhir

aligned menhirs

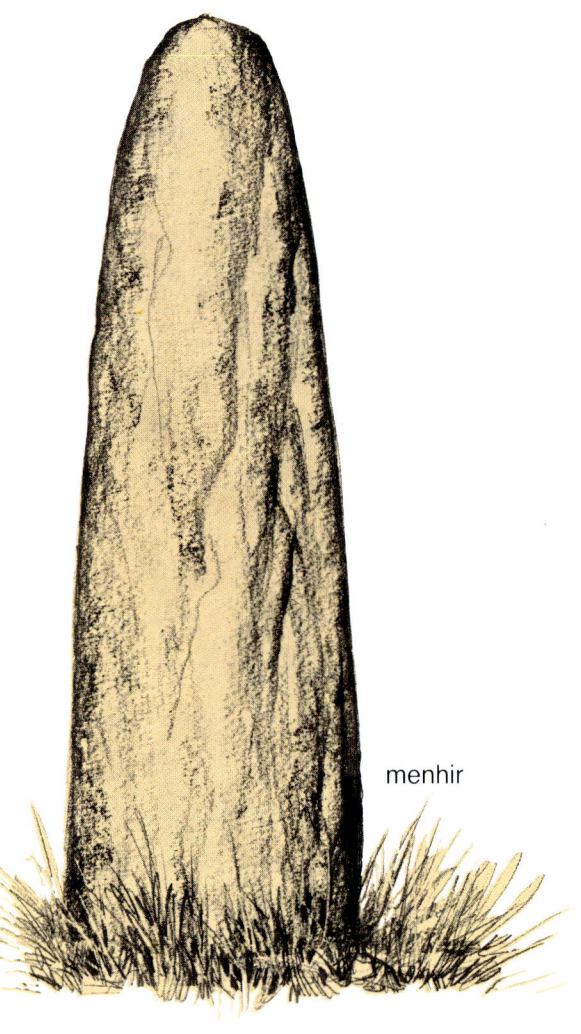

cromlech

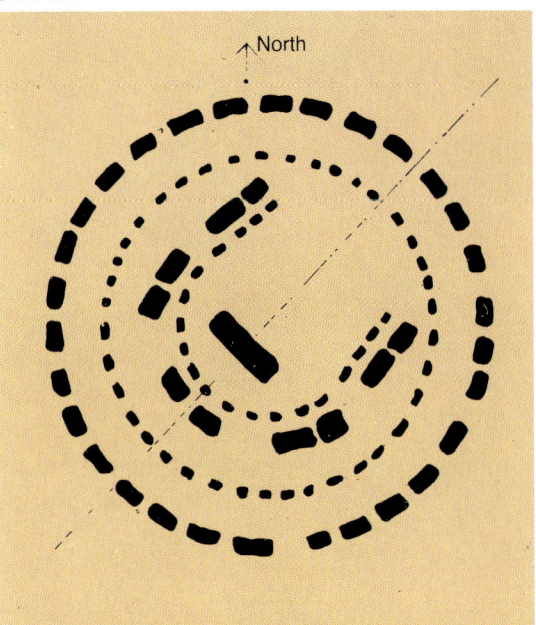

↑North

The ground plan shown above reproduces the circular site of Stonehenge during the peak of its development. The outermost of the four circles was formed by monoliths (single stone blocks) which supported a continuous line of lintels (horizontal pieces). One of the two inner circles that opened towards the entrance was formed of five huge blocks or triliths (two vertical blocks topped by a horizontal block). The transport and placement of these rocks, which are up to 50 tonnes in weight, required an enormous amount of work, a sophisticated ability to calculate, and technical skill.

Some scholars call the monument a solar temple and suggest the idea that Stonehenge was used for astronomical observation of the heavens as well as the prediction of eclipses of the sun.

Priest-astronomers gathered on the day of the summer solstice observe the sun as it rises in perfect alignment with the axis of the entrance to the Stonehenge monument.

THE GREAT STONES—MONUMENTS TO THE HUMAN COMMUNITY

The Megaliths

At the end of the Neolithic period and during the beginning of the Bronze Age, humans began living in villages and so strengthened social ties. Monuments called megaliths date back to this time and range from before 4000 B.C. to soon after 2000 B.C. *Megalith* is a word of Greek origin meaning "large stone." Besides being proof of great architectural skill, these stones were also evidence of organized, collective work. Megaliths are found in different shapes throughout the world and are numerous throughout Europe, reaching impressive densities in some regions. There are different types of megaliths. The menhir megaliths stand isolated. The aligned megaliths are in a row. The cromlech megaliths are placed in a circle. The dolmen consists of two or more upright stones supporting a horizontal stone slab.

Menhir, Aligned Megaliths, and Cromlech

Menhir is a word coming from the Breton language meaning "long stone." In fact, these are stone blocks which can reach over 20 metres in height. They stand on end, set into the ground, and are left uncarved. Sometimes these rocks are not isolated, but instead are found in groups which are placed in parallel rows (aligned megaliths). In France at Carnacit, it is possible to observe a row of megaliths stretching for 4 km, composed of 2,934 stone blocks. Scholars believe that these blocks were erected for religious purposes.

The word *cromlech* also comes from the Breton language and has the dual meaning of "curved" and "stone." The most perfect cromlech example is at the site of Stonehenge on Salisbury Plain in Great Britain. This complex was built in three different stages. At first, around 2000 B.C., a 90 metre circular area was surrounded by a ditch. Within this area, 56 pits were dug. The circle was interrupted on the southeast side by the entrance to the area, which was marked with a menhir. Two centuries later, numerous blocks of blue stone (either deposited on the site by glaciation or transported from 200 km away) were erected to form a double circle. Finally, a few years later, the most monumental stage of development took place. More large blocks were added, transported from a nearby area. The final complex was formed of four concentric circles. The two innermost circles opened in the shape of a horseshoe, corresponding to the entrance.

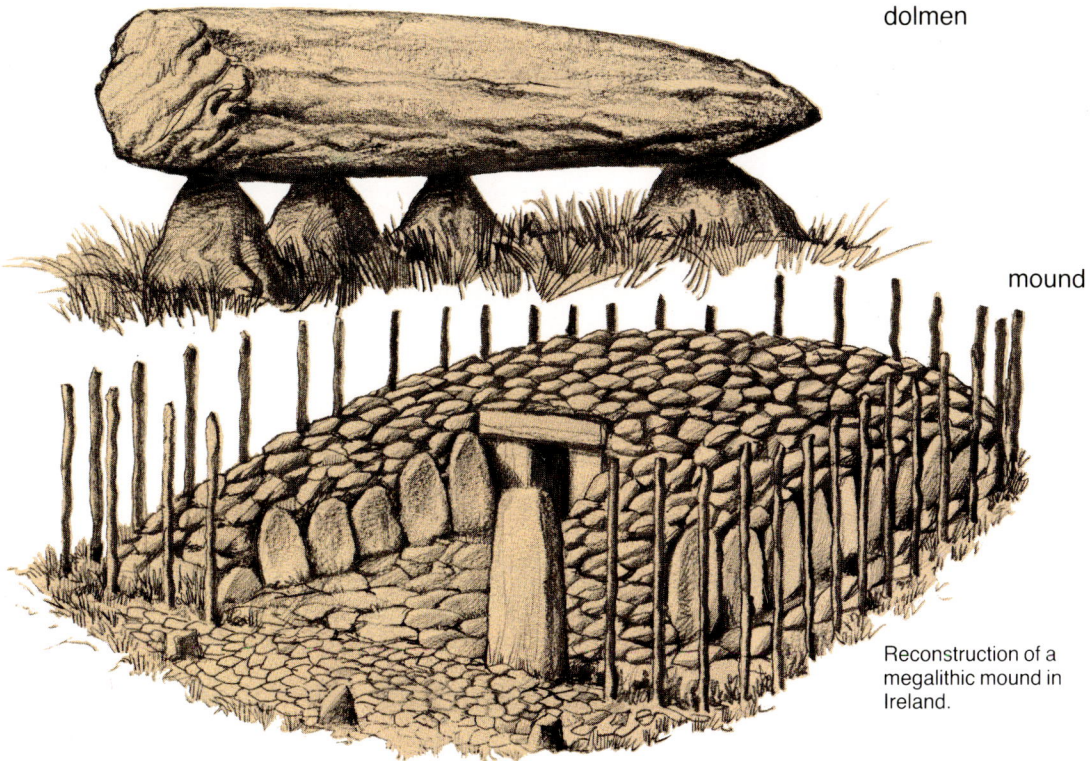

Dolmens and Mounds

The dolmen is distinguished from the other kinds of megaliths because it is the only one that has a clear function. Usually, it marks a collective tomb. This monument also symbolizes the solidarity of a village. The inhabitants of a village took care to gather all the dead of the clan into the same tomb. *Dolmen* is a word derived from the Breton language which means "stone slab." In fact, the most simple dolmens were formed of a slab set on top of two pillars. The space thus obtained was a burial chamber which was often covered with stones or dirt to form a mound. Some dolmens were only burial chambers, while others were also furnished with a hallway or other assorted chambers.

Many variations exist in different regions, and sometimes dolmens are associated with various kinds of megaliths. For example, there are cromlech surrounding dolmens which are covered by a mound. In Sardinia, cromlech and aligned megaliths can be part of the same tomb. The common element in all these variations is the great care with which these burial monuments were built. The monuments are sacred places where the dead were placed with careful respect, accompanied by personal objects such as vases, tools, and weapons. At times, walls and supporting columns were richly decorated. Some walls were so densely carved that not even an inch of stone was left untouched. The interpretation of these carved symbols is not completely clear, but their patterns and precision suggest great symbolic significance.

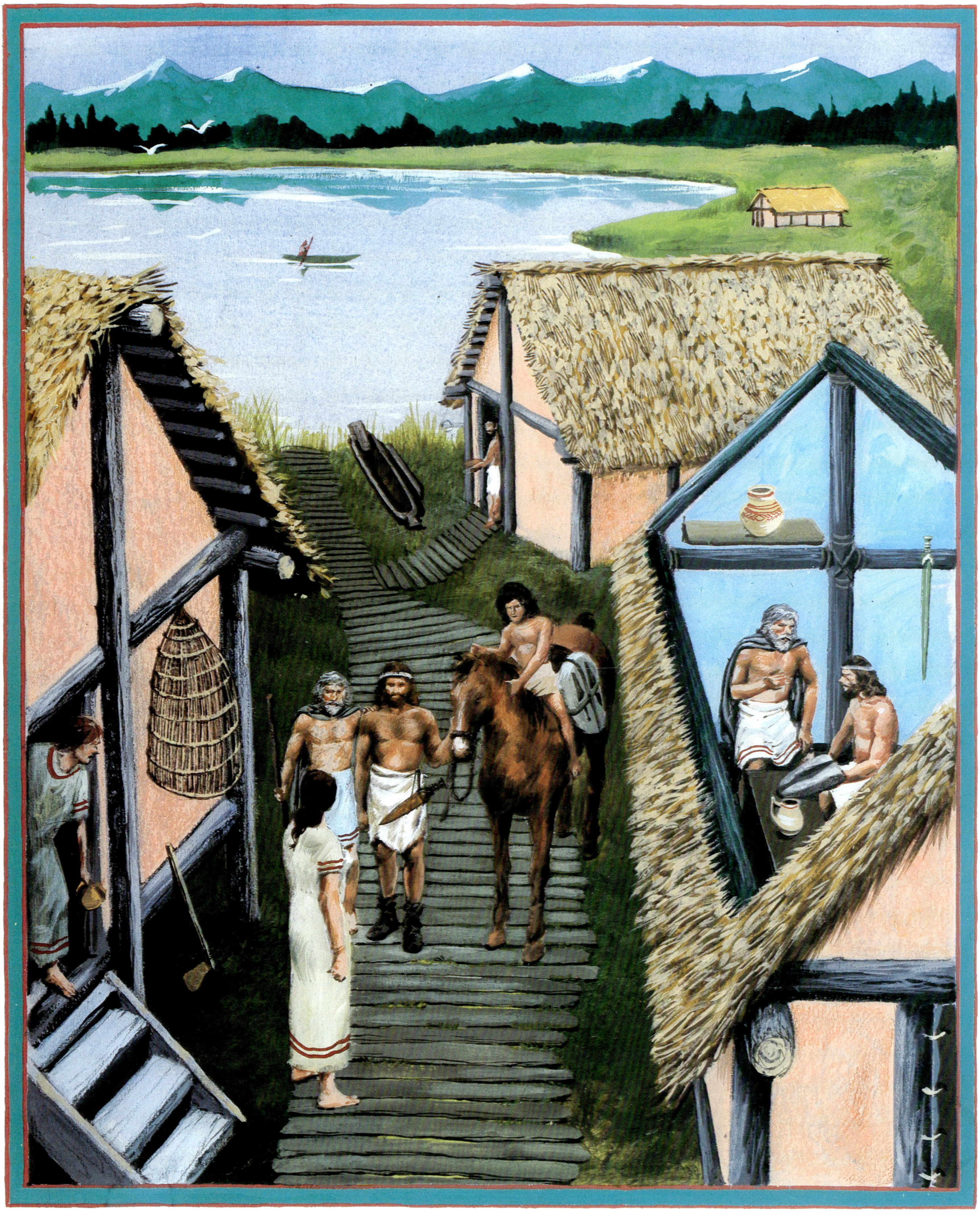

BRONZE ARRIVES IN EUROPE

The Growth of European Populations

In the second half of the third millennium B.C., Europe became increasingly crowded. Some regions in particular were quite heavily populated. In certain areas, population densities increased ten-fold. The sizes of villages greatly increased. Hundreds of people, sometimes belonging to dozens of families, were grouped in the villages and lived in dense clusters of houses. Migration and increases in human populations had another result. Frequent contact between people caused rapid distribution of innovations, customs, experiences, and ideas. It also increased the level of tension between different groups, creating competition and even wars.

Bronze Work and Travelling Smiths

Metal played a large role in economic and social change. Starting around 2500 B.C., the first types of bronze, obtained by adding arsenic or antimony to copper, spread through most of Europe. Finally, the best hardening agent for copper was discovered—tin. Tin was an easy metal to use because its melting point was low, but unfortunately it was quite rare.

Travelling smiths offered their services from town to town. On their horses, they carried the moulds which were used for the manufacture of different tools. The arrival of the smith was an important event for the village because people were always in need of new tools and weapons.

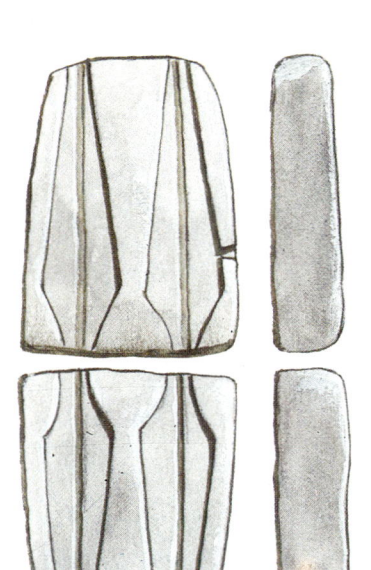

The smiths of Mesopotamia and Anatolia learned how to mix copper with small quantities of tin (not over 10 per cent) even before 3000 B.C. The European smiths arrived at the same conclusions independently later. In this way, a truer bronze was created.

The task of working the new metal was difficult and required great skill and hard work. It was not an activity meant for everyone. Also, supplying the minerals required the existence of complex commercial channels and even the creation of political relationships between different populations or their leaders. Some people in each population specialized in this new skill, backed and possibly even supported by the community or the leaders. Until the period of the late Bronze Age, traces of permanent village forges are very sparse.

Front and side views of moulds for casting bronze.

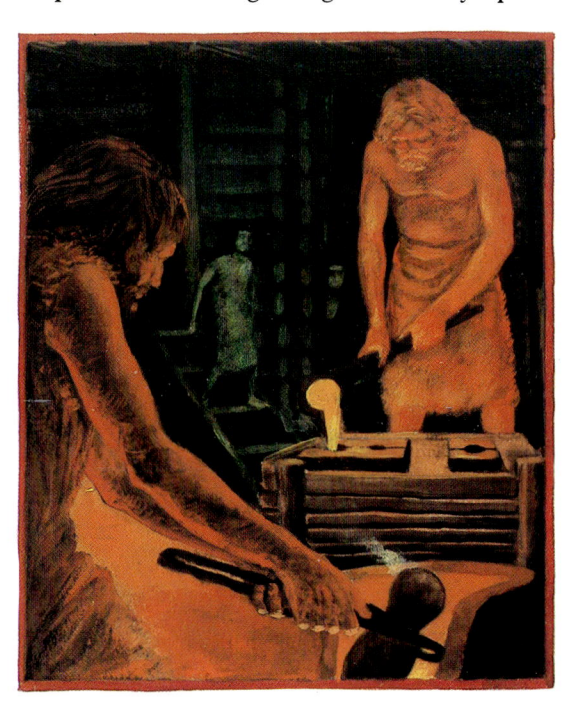

A smith pours melted bronze into moulds.

Far right: **1)** An enlarged detail of a gold pin **2)** An axe head **3)** A pin for a robe **4)** A ceramic cup decorated with graphite.

Smiths were travelling technicians who would assemble their forges in the various villages where they stopped. They carried their casting moulds and their bags full of raw metal with them. They passed on their skills to their children. Metalworking was the beginning of industrial activity. With the smelting of bronze, multiple copies of objects could be produced. The casting moulds were used time and time again.

The Religious Role of Smiths

All artisans, miners and smiths in particular, felt that they were a part of nature. Minerals were seen as the result of a process of ripening or a slow process of birth. Miners and smiths were people who could facilitate and expedite the process of birth for their new products. Whoever carried out this type of work was also performing activities of a religious kind which had to be preceded by rituals. The job of a smith called into action some of the most secret forces of nature. Smiths were sought after and respected but also feared, and for this reason had to live outside the community.

The skills for this work were either orally transmitted or learned through apprenticeship. European artisans taught their skills to their children. Techniques were handed down and not affected by the political or social climate of the communities. Such techniques were preserved until the late Middle Ages.

The main area for working copper was located in the southeastern region. Bronze was mainly produced in central Europe. The first bronze smelters appeared in Bohemia, near naturally occurring deposits of copper and tin.

There is evidence that these local smiths were skilled in the art of producing copper mixed with arsenic. This pioneer culture, which developed around 2300 B.C., has been given the name of Unetice. Within three or four generations, other centres appeared in Hungary, Yugoslavia, and Bavaria near the deposits of the Austrian Alps, in the Swiss Valley, and in the Rhone region of France.

Two-sided moulds allowed for the production of a number of new tools, mostly derived from the Chalcolithic (early Bronze Age) patterns of production. Among them were triangular daggers with heavy handles, axes for battle as well as for wood chopping, long pins, bracelets, and jewellery of varied shapes. The most peculiar pieces were probably open collars which became valued objects and were used as the first type of European currency.

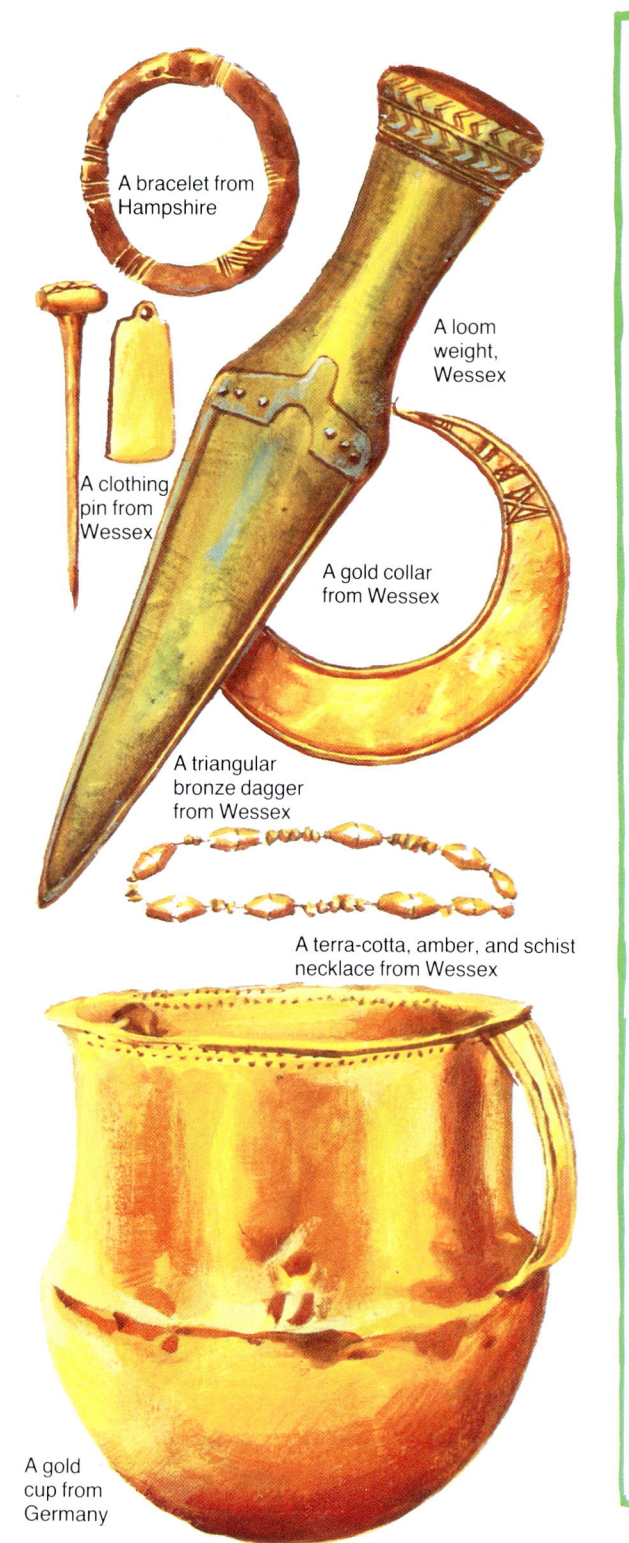

LIFE IN THE BRONZE AGE
From 2300 to 1300 B.C.

Food Products

The Bronze Age was a period of time when bronze was used to make tools and weapons. It was the time between the Stone Age and the Iron Age. The Bronze Age was a time of abundance in Europe. Never before was locally produced food so varied and plentiful. Each community was able to sustain itself on its own crops. In the third millennium, pigs began to be raised. This was an adaptation to the mixed oak forest which covered Europe. In the second millennium, the raising of cattle spread and improved. These primitive animal rearing techniques involved small, sturdy stock. The farmers employed heavy ploughs and good quality scythes with flint blades.

Transport

Wheeled vehicles began to be used over different parts of the continent. The most important transport animal was the ox.

Clothing

During this period, men and women were increasingly well clothed. Experimentation with wool took place in scattered areas and probably appeared in the Balkan regions and in Italy in the third millennium. Spinning and weaving greatly improved at the same time, due to the creation of specific tools and the

In a village, a new house is being built using bronze axes. A man on his way back from the fields carries a plough. *Right:* Various members of the community had different tasks and degrees of power. This is an indication of differentiation within society.

The leader assured trade, controlled wealth, and defended the community. The prince in this illustration is wearing a massive gold collar.

The priest offered sacrifices. He allowed the community to maintain its relationship with the gods.

The artisan-merchant knew the secrets of metalworking. He produced and traded prized objects used for practical uses and personal ornamentation.

The farmer worked the land and produced food for the entire community.

selection of breeds of sheep and goats with a softer wool. All of the different peoples rapidly took to wearing clothing made with light or dark wool or with linen decorated with woven patterns and fringes.

The wealthiest people started to dress with sparkling bronze buttons. The appearance of people changed as they began to embellish their basic clothing with items such as brooches.

The Differentiation of Society

The Bronze Age brought major changes in social life. The total population was no longer dedicated to farming and livestock raising. In addition to farmers and shepherds who produced food for the community, others endowed with particular skills created differences in wealth and power. The interest in copper and bronze prompted people to desire some types of minerals which were not found in every region, as well as objects which only a few artisans knew how to make.

Whoever had control of mineral traffic and could protect the merchants and members of the community could become a leader and gain political power over other people and land. The artisan-merchants who knew the skill of metalworking and merchants who specialized in trade had important positions in the community. Additionally, the carrying out of sacrifices was assigned to particular men, the priests. The sacrifice of animals was meant to keep communication open between the community and the gods. This task was believed to be essential, and the power of the priests was as great as that of the political leaders.

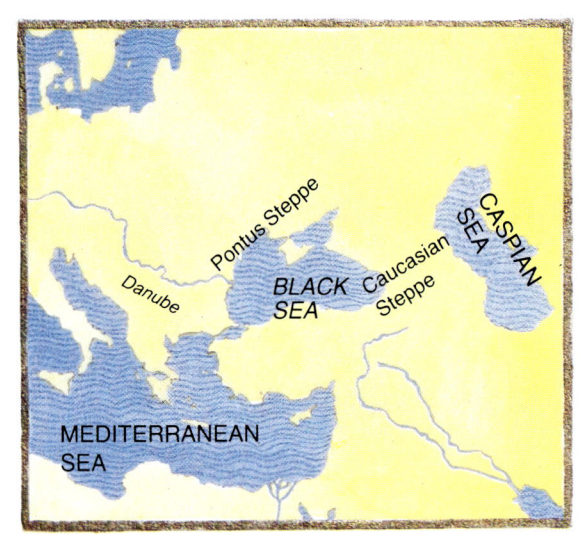

Around the third and second millennia B.C., the Eurasian herding communities began to put pressure on Europe from the east and expanded westward.

This representation of a sailing vessel on a seal dates from 2000 B.C.

PROFESSIONAL TRAVELLERS

The second millennium B.C. was a time of great mobility. The Mediterranean shores were systematically navigated, and people also explored the Atlantic coasts and inland stretches of water. Riding horses became widespread in most regions, and wheeled wagons were commonly used.

The Sea Routes

In the second millennium, the boats of the Aegean Sea were equipped with square sails, while in the stormy northern seas, they continued to be propelled by oars. Certainly the use of sails made possible open sea navigation, but sailors preferred to hug the shores or use sea channels with land always in sight. Narrow passages along rocky coasts had stopping points for the navigators to spend the night. Travel was rarely done at night by sea or by land. The Lipari Islands and Sardinia, which were the islands where obsidian (a black rock used for making tools) was found, had been the destination of expeditions since the early years of the Neolithic period. The Tyrrhenian obsidian routes ran near the coasts of Calabria and southern Campania and passed the Isle of Elba. The distribution of several types of obsidian, found both in Italy and southern France, corresponds to these routes.

The two shores of the Adriatic Sea had been united by a common culture since the Mesolithic period. An important early route even before the beginning of the Bronze Age extended north along the Adriatic Sea from the western Greek islands to Dalmatia and the outlet of the Po River, passing through the straights of Otranto between Albania and Italy. Amber from Denmark and the Baltic

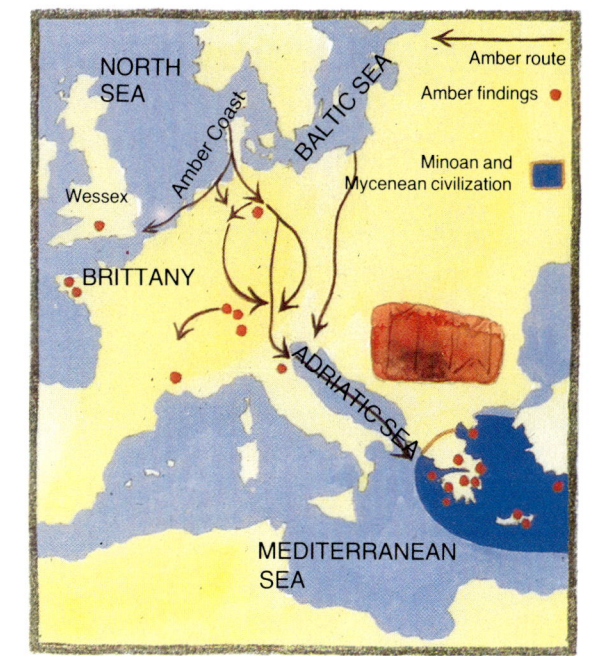

The "amber route" carried precious amber tree sap from the North Sea all the way to the Adriatic Sea and the eastern Mediterranean.

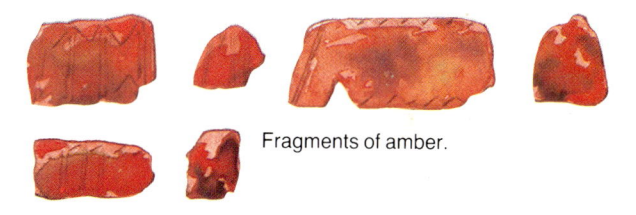

Fragments of amber.

Opposite page: Foreign traders land in a cove on a Mediterranean island to trade their goods.

Far left: Navigation of inland waters such as rivers and lakes was highly developed.

Left: The ridden horse became a widespread means of transport, allowing people to move rapidly from place to place.

region reached the lagoons at the northern end of the gulf through a land route. From there it was sent by sea to the Mediterranean markets and later to the city-states of the Mycenaean civilization.

In the last centuries of the second millennium, the populations of the Apulian Apennines in southern Italy and Mycenae together controlled the trading centres in the Gulf of Tarentum at the southernmost point of the Italian peninsula. The Tyrrhenian route was, on the other hand, under the control of the Apenninian people who inhabited the central and southern regions of Italy. The final destination for these southern populations was probably the metal deposits in Tuscany and on the Isle of Elba. Along the coast of Italy, the various settlements left their marks on Greek tradition. For example, they were mentioned in the tales of the travels of the Argonauts and the deeds of Ulysses.

The Horse

The horse was the best means of transport on the European continent during the Bronze Age. Besides carrying goods and people, the horse was also a means of spreading language, culture, and ideas. The horse was considered a symbol of speed and mobility. For this reason, it was regarded by the Indo-Europeans as a mark of prestige and nobility. Horses were even buried with their owners.

THE ORIGIN OF EUROPEAN PEOPLE

During the last part of the Bronze Age, which extended from 1300 B.C. to 700 B.C., the results of the technological revolution were highly evident in Europe. There were more and more people, requiring more land to farm, new methods of cultivation, and new plants. Rye was a newly discovered grain. There was a need for a new social organization.

The Rise of the Privileged Classes

One of the main changes caused by the discovery of bronze was the differentiation and specialization of people. Some people became skilled in metalworking, others traded artifacts, some would invest their skills in accumulating wealth, and some leaders organized the work of the whole group and sold the products to others. In this way, some people became more privileged than others. This is demonstrated in the Bronze Age by the existence of tombs of the wealthy, clearly different from those of the poor.

Long Distance Trade

From the Neolithic period onwards, people organized their commercial exchanges. During the Bronze Age, there was a marked increase in the trade of obsidian, amber, stone, and seashells. The metal trade prompted the creation of workshops to produce artifacts for sale at home and in distant lands.

Villages Begin to Resemble Towns

The number of weapons which have been found in the excavation sites of the Bronze Age has led scholars to speculate that, at least toward the end of the period, this was an age of instability. Evidence of this is also found in the number of fortifications which were built on the hills dating back to the same period.

Warfare must have been widely practised during this period of major movement of populations. It has never been made clear whether the groups of newcomers were peaceful merchants or conquerors attracted by fertile land or precious resources. An example of defensive activity is the nuraghe from the Sardinian civilization. Nuraghes were towers built on elevated sites for observation and defence. Eventually additional towers and surrounding walls were added, and the buildings became more like castles.

A Religious Spirit in Search of Symbols

In the art of this time, a disc representing the sun was often carved on rocks and was often surrounded by human figures in prayer stances. During this time, study and respect for the stars became widespread, almost as if humankind were seeking something which could be considered a symbol of eternal life. Human beings worshipped the stars and the

This bronze and gold chariot found in Denmark was used in cult rituals. It has a representation of the sun (the highest cosmic god of the Bronze Age) being drawn through the sky by a horse.

These bronze statuettes found in Denmark represent people in prayer.

Below: A view of a Sardinian village with a nuraghe, or watch tower.

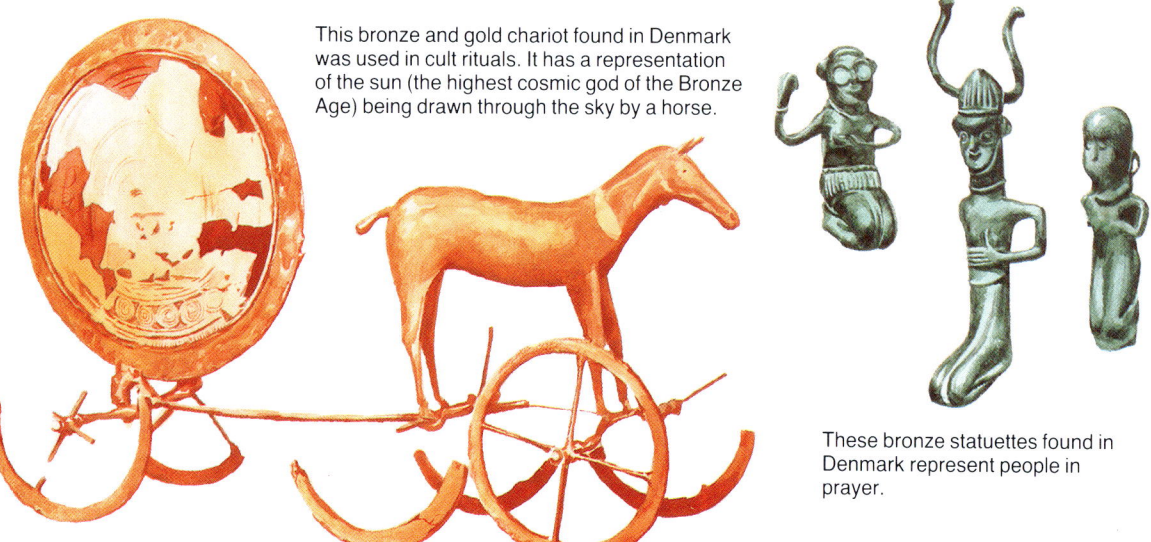

Above are funerary urns from northern Germany used for the burial of the ashes of the dead. This new ritual suddenly and rapidly spread through most of Europe during the last period of the Bronze Age.

Merchants from the Aegean Sea on their arrival at an Alpine village, where they will trade their goods.

Burial in urns, however, did not completely replace the funerary rituals which already existed. The above illustration shows a mound found in western Germany. The mound provided protection for the body of the dead. Inside, some of the objects owned by the dead were arranged to accompany them into the next life and as offerings to the gods.

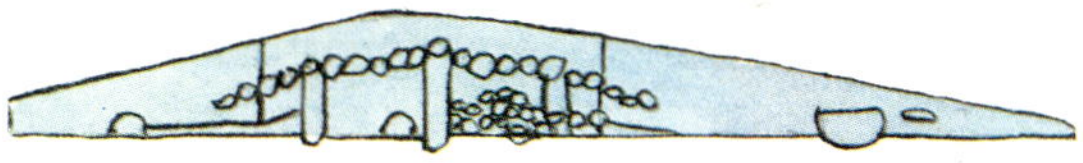

Above is a cross section of a mound found in Switzerland which dates back to 2500 B.C. The burial chamber is covered with stones and then with soil to create the mound, or barrow.

earth, from whose womb flowed water, the source of all life. The sacred sites were outdoors. In fact, large quantities of precious objects, weapons, and prayer offerings were found close to rivers and springs, in woods and caves, and sometimes in sacred enclosures.

At the same time, a new funerary ritual began to spread surprisingly rapidly—cremation. The ashes of the dead were placed in urns which were buried in rows in vast fields. With the start of this new ritual, a change in the conception of the afterlife can be sensed. Attempts were no longer made to preserve the body, but instead it was destroyed by cremation so that the spirit of the dead could rise to heaven.

35

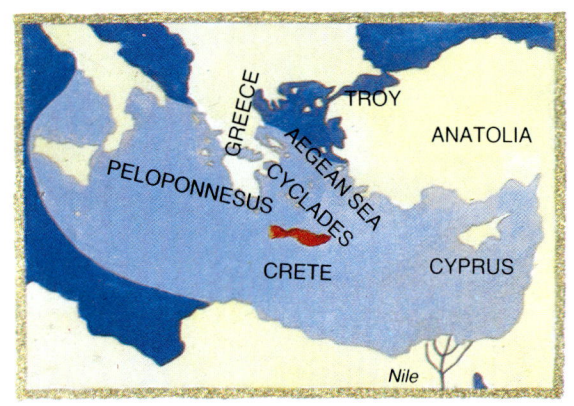

Crete is like a bridge, extending both into the Aegean and eastern Mediterranean seas. Goods and artisans were regularly sent to Egypt and the Near East.

These axes are miniature prayer objects. In fact, the finding of real weapons is rare in Crete. The axes measure 8 cm across. They were found in a cave in the central part of the island at Arkalochori.

Above is a reconstruction of the inner courtyard of the palace of Knossos. Below is an overall view. The palace stretched over 19,000 square metres.

THE GOLDEN AGE OF CRETE

The Aegean Lands: A Bridge Between Asia and Europe

The lands on the Aegean Sea share the same climate, soil, and natural resources. They also share the same body of water which, in every epoch, was a means of communication between Asia, Europe, and North Africa through which ideas, technology, and goods were transported. These lands were subject to various influences, and this has aroused discussion among scholars about the origins of the civilizations which developed in these areas. However, one of these civilizations was so unique that all of the possible influences which might have shaped it are of secondary importance. This was the civilization of Crete.

Today, the island of Crete appears barren and dry, but in ancient times it was famous for its pastures, vineyards, olive groves, and oak and cypress woods. However, it was poor in mineral resources, and its geographical location was not as favourable as that of Cyprus, which was in the midst of sea routes. Thus, the splendour which Crete achieved during the Bronze Age was surprising.

Between 2000 and 1570 B.C., Crete was the site of a refined civilization. Knossos was, in fact, the first real city in Europe.

Large, similar palaces are also found elsewhere in Europe, but those of Crete have a unique feature. They are open to the air, and they exude a sense of peace in sharp contrast with what was found, for example, in Mycenae. This peaceful nature had a major effect on the development of art and culture.

A Civilization With Writing

Writing had been in use in Crete since the founding of the first palaces. This early form of writing has been found painted on vases and carved on stone and clay. It is a type of picture-writing in which a symbolic drawing indicates an entire word.

From around 1800 B.C., another kind of writing came into use in which a sign corres-

This object is part of a painted coffin found in Ayia Triadha in the southern part of Crete. It dates from 1400 B.C. and depicts humans carrying gifts to a man standing in front of his own tomb.

One of the thousands of inscribed clay tablets from the palace at Knossos. Its writings date from 1400 B.C.

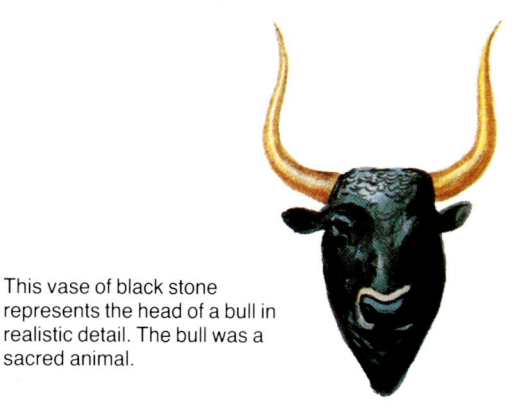

This vase of black stone represents the head of a bull in realistic detail. The bull was a sacred animal.

First Discoveries in Crete

The British archaeologist Arthur Evans (1851-1941), was the first to conduct excavations of the Cretan palaces and to discover abundant evidence of this civilization. At the end of the last century, he travelled in Greece and was fascinated by the excavation of Mycenae which was being carried out by the German archaeologist Heinrich Schliemann. Evans arrived in Crete, where he became interested in the writing found there. He was also attracted by objects that women wore around their necks, which had carved symbols similar to hieroglyphics. He bought a piece of land which had been selected by Schliemann for its potential and began excavations. He uncovered two palaces, one being the palace of Knossos.

ponded to the sound of a syllable. This was mainly used concerning objects of religious significance, and it was in use only in Crete. Still another kind of writing was added later, and within the island was used only at Knossos. It was also used outside Crete in Greece. It was decoded, and even though it is not completely understood, it has been recognized as being similar to the Greek language.

The Religion of the Cretans

The absence of large temples to accompany such superb palaces is surprising. The Cretan people instead erected outdoor altars, both in the rural areas and in town. The domestic and family side of spirituality was stressed. Representations of human figures in praying postures were common, and unlike in Egypt, the statues of the deities are small. Cretan religion was expressed in ritual dance and in paintings. These works often featured bulls and snakes. The bull was considered sacred.

The Fate of Crete and Its Palaces

The great buildings of Crete were destroyed several times. The first time was around 1700 B.C., the probable cause an earthquake. Later, the palaces were rebuilt, but were again destroyed in 1450 B.C. from unknown causes. Knossos was unharmed. It was occupied and restored by invaders coming from the mainland. But shortly after in approximately 1400 B.C., it was completely destroyed.

THE BRONZE AGE—CIVILIZATION OF THE GREEK MAINLAND

In approximately 1600 B.C., prosperous centres of activity developed on the Greek mainland. The most famous was Mycenae, but Tiryns, Thebes, Athens, and Pylos also became important. The Cretan civilization was still in existence, but most of it was rapidly being absorbed by the Greek mainland which developed a completely new civilization.

Warriors with Rich Tombs

Even though recent discoveries have been made in other sites, there is evidence that the beginning and early development of ancient Greek civilization took place only in the town of Mycenae. The finding of two burial areas on a hill in Mycenae has provided evidence of the lives of the men and women who lived and were buried there. The first area was discovered by Schliemann in 1876 and dated back to 1550 and 1500 B.C. The second area was excavated in the 1950s by Greek archaeologists and contains even earlier remains.

Spectacular treasures were preserved in circular enclosures surrounded by rocks at the entrances of tombs. The bodies of the dead were richly dressed and adorned with finely crafted gold ornaments. They had gold masks over their faces. The quantity and quality of precious objects must have left the first discoverers breathless. On the objects which accompanied the bodies were scenes of hunting and of violent fighting, quite distinct from the peaceful motifs of Crete. Women were buried wearing marvellous jewels, and men rested with their swords and daggers at their sides. The elaborate costumes and the magnificent artifacts suggest that these people had great power in their society.

Kings and Monumental Burials

Society of this time (1300 B.C.) in Mycenae was ruled by kings who lived in fortresses. These fortresses were not surrounded by actual towns but by villages inhabited by farmers and artisans. The manual labour used by the royal dynasties to complete their great works of construction mainly came from the practice of piracy, which provided slaves. Plentiful riches came from trading and agriculture. The warrior kings of Mycenae during this time probably sailed through the part of the Aegean Sea which separated the defenceless palaces of Crete from their territories. They easily conquered this desirable jewel of the sea. Also during this period, Greek merchants travelled extensively. They reached southern Italy, the Syrian coast, and even England.

The size of the fortress where the ruler of this society lived is impressive. The walls of Mycenae reached a width of 4.5 metres and a height of 15 metres. The walls of Tiryns were so thick that a tunnel was built through them. The palaces were designed with different features from those of Crete. The ground plan was more strictly defined, and its centre was called a megaron. These palaces were formed of a series of rooms in a rectangular space, with a long throne room and a lobby decorated with columns.

The palace of Pylos is the best preserved and has been recently excavated by an American expedition. It consists of two blocks of buildings, one residential on two levels and another

At the top is a gold death mask found in one of the shaft graves in Mycenae. It dates from 1500 B.C. Above are two examples of Mycenaean armour. That on the left is made of leather and is from 1200 B.C. The other is made of bronze and is from 1400 B.C.

Above: Part of the lobby of the palace of Pylos, built in 1300 B.C. and destroyed by a great fire in 1200 B.C. Below is a gold cup, probably the work of a Cretan artisan, found in one of the tombs of Mycenae from 1500 B.C.

This illustration shows a piece of pottery found at Tiryns depicting Greek warriors. Some experts connect these figures with the Sea People, raiders depicted in the Egyptian bas-reliefs.

The Acheans

In the epic literature of later times, the Greek populations are called Acheans. There have been many discussions over whether this name might coincide with the name of *akhkhiyawa*, who were mentioned as raiders in Hittite documents. (The Hittites built a kingdom in Anatolia, which is Turkey today.) It has been decided that the word means Acheans, but there is no proof that the Acheans could be identified with the warrior kings of Mycenae and with other towns of the Greek world. Surprisingly similar words are also used by the Egyptians to define the Sea People who carried out several raids on the Nile Delta, but there is no proof that these people were Greek.

The poems of Homer indicate that the Acheans were responsible for the siege of Troy in Anatolia, but although Mycenaean objects were found during excavation, there is no evidence that the events coincided. Thus, the identity of the Acheans mentioned in the documents of 1200 B.C. still remains a mystery, as does the role of the Greeks in the complex events of the Near East.

one for administration. It is built of stone and wood, and the most important rooms are painted. The burial sites of these kings were of monumental size.

The so-called thalos tombs were named after a Greek word meaning circular construction. The most well preserved tomb was found in Mycenae. It is a round burial chamber dug into the rock with a diameter of 15 metres, and its entrance is beautifully decorated. This chamber is reached through a long passageway. It is a monument to the power of a king who ruled Mycenae in approximately 1250 B.C. He is buried with his family.

The Last Great Catastrophe

There was a warlike attitude prevalent during these times. Attacks from the outside and internal instability were constant. Only a few dynasties were able to endure and con-

Troops march in front of the fortified citadel of Mycenae. This illustration shows its probable appearance in approximately 1250 B.C.

tinue to rule their territories. Mycenae, Tiryns and Thebes show traces of extensive ruins, followed by new and sturdier fortifications. Around 1200 B.C., most of the fortresses and palaces were finally demolished throughout Greece. After this, these sites remained inhabited, but none of the palaces were ever rebuilt and their political and administrative significance disappeared from Greek tradition.

It is thought that the Dorian populations may have been responsible for the destruction. Another theory suggests that a coalition known as the "Sea People" was responsible.

The only certainty is that there was an invasion from the north, which caused complete and tremendous social change. The society of the palaces had been destroyed, and a new one was about to rise.

The natural features of the Mediterranean habitat played a major role in the lives of the Greek populations during the dark centuries. They drew all their necessary resources from the surrounding territory. On top of the hill is one of the first temples, which were built towards the end of this period.

THE "DARK CENTURIES" OF GREECE

Great Changes

The collapse of the Mycenaean civilization around 1200 B.C. caused impoverishment and was followed by what is commonly called "the dark centuries" from the twelfth to the ninth centuries B.C. These centuries were called dark for the people who lived then because one world had ended, and another one was slowly starting to emerge. The archaeological finds give the impression of a monotonous environment. Human and animal representations were no longer found, stone construction became rare, precious stones were no longer used, and gold was hardly ever present. Luxury imports disappeared, and warriors were buried surrounded only by a few lance points. Cremation of the dead was practised, and the ashes were buried in urns.

The Migrations

During this time, migrations took place that brought the Greek populations into new settlements on the islands of the Aegean Sea and on the coast of Asia Minor. The migrating groups settled in separate nuclei and, as a result of a lack of trade and a scarcity of farmland, were small in size. Villages were built with tightly clustered houses and were often protected by walls. Each village dominated a small territory from which it drew most of its necessary resources. Each nucleus was independent of the others and was inhabited by a different tribe. Communications mainly occurred by sea along the coast.

Technology and Iron

Once the economic importance of trade by

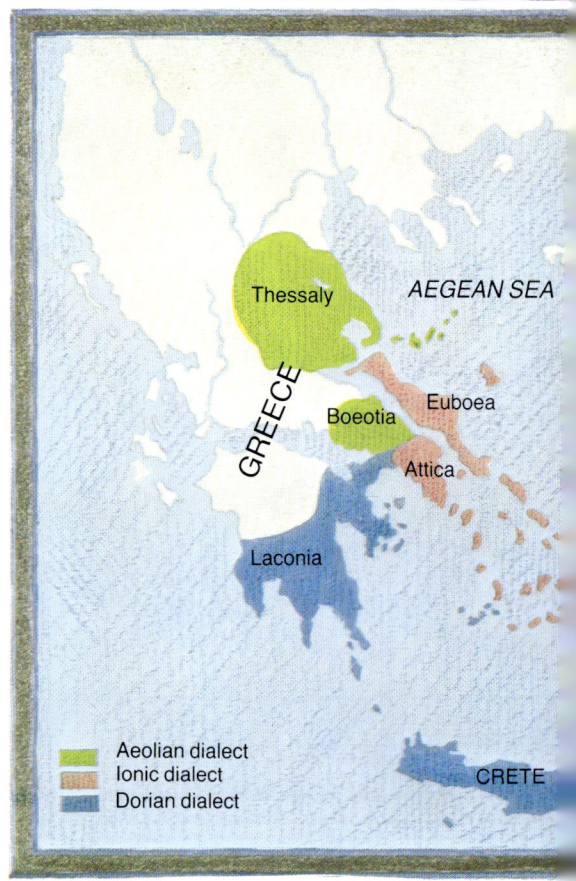

The spread of Greek dialects indicates patterns of migration of the Greek populations to the coasts of Asia Minor, between the 12th and 9th centuries B.C.

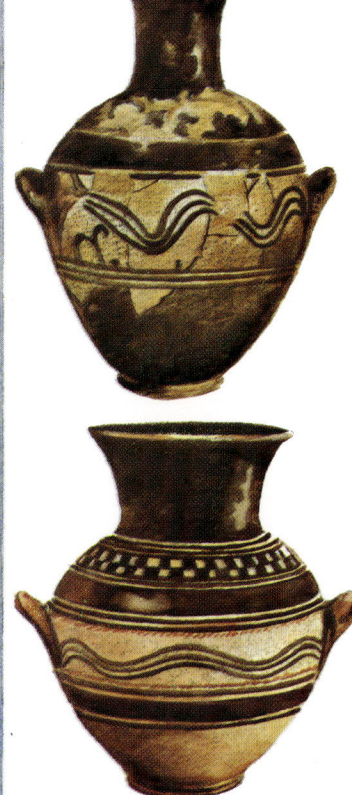

sea decreased, the more traditional activities of production became dominant. Agriculture and livestock turned Greece into a country of fields and flocks. However, during this epoch, an important technological change took place—the spread of ironwork that had been introduced from the Anatolian region. Preceding other European populations, the Greeks acquired a marked degree of skill in methods of metal production. Iron was harder than bronze and was used for the manufacture of swords, spears, daggers, rings, pins and clasps. At a later time, iron was also used to improve working and farming tools. The ceramics of this period were decorated with geometric patterns.

The Domestic Economy

Economic activities were focused around the home. Both agriculture and animal raising mainly served the needs of the inhabitants of the village. Oil was produced, wheat was ground into flour, wool was combed and woven, all of the tools necessary for work were produced, as well as clothing, furniture and footwear.

Social Organization

All the inhabitants of a village, except slaves, were related by blood. Each person with civil rights belonged to a genos, which was a group of immediate descendants from a single individual. The genos was part of the fratriat, which was the group of all the descendants from a common ancestor. The fratriats joined together forming tribes. Within each tribe existed some prominent families who had greater wealth and formed the aristocracy of the village. Above the aristocracy, there was a leader who inherited the title of chief. Finally, above everyone else there was another king of the largest settlement who ruled several tribes with the help of a council of elders. This king had special authority and a special function. He was the religious chief, and the fertility of the fields and animals as well as the prosperity of his subjects depended on him.

These ceramic vases with geometric decorations date from the 11th and 10th centuries B.C.

41

IN THE "DARK CENTURIES", POEMS TOLD OF A HEROIC AGE

Homer and Oral Poetry

Two of the most important epic poems of the Western world were written during the dark centuries. The *Iliad* and the *Odyssey* narrate the life and deeds of two legendary heroes of ancient Greece, Achilles and Odysseus. These two poems are the culmination of an ancient oral tradition, by which heroic stories were passed on by memory from generation to generation by Greek poets and singers. Works of this type were given their final form in writing in Ionia between the eighth and seventh centuries B.C. by the poet Homer. He is credited with writing the *Iliad* and the *Odyssey* although scholars have doubts about the specific period in which he lived, about his origins, and even about his very existence.

The *Iliad*

Achilles, according to ancient legends, was dipped into the waters of a river, the Styx, by his mother in an effort to make him invulnerable. His only vulnerable point was his heel, where his mother grasped him during the immersion. As the king of the tribe of the Tessalies, he went to war against the city of Troy. The prince of Troy, Paris, abducted Helen, the wife of Menelaus, the king of Sparta. Many of the Greek towns, led by their kings, declared war on Troy to avenge the crime. After nine years of siege and heroic fighting, Troy was destroyed.

The *Odyssey*

Odysseus, king of the island of Ithaca, was also involved in the Trojan War, and the *Odyssey* tells of his adventures during his long journey home. He was protected by the goddess Athena and came across deities and monsters but always succeeded in overcoming any difficulties. Upon his arrival in Ithaca, he killed the nobles who had seized the throne during his absence and re-established order under his own authority. Odysseus, more so than Achilles, developed into a famous myth in western culture. Great skill and strength were part of his character. But Odysseus was also clever. He built the famous wooden horse which deceived the Trojans. The fantastic adventures of Odysseus's journey still fascinate readers in modern times.

The Gods of Homer

The world of Homer was organized on two levels—the earth, where people developed their society, and Mount Olympus, which was the sacred mountain and dwelling place of the gods. The organization of the gods' world was very similar to that of human society. For example, the leader of the people was the king, and the leader of the gods was Zeus, who was father and lord of both humans and gods. The gods were immortal and had a great deal of power, a valued quality in the Greek world. Gods were not perfect and omnipotent. Each one of them excelled at only one particular task. The relationship between gods and people was very close: Achilles and Odysseus are constantly guided or hindered by the gods during their adventures.

Heroic Ideal

The two protagonists of the Homeric poems were heroes. In the Greek world, a hero wishes to live life to the fullest, enjoying all of the opportunities offered, totally immersed in the present. The ideal is to bring the characteristics given by nature as close to perfection as possible. According to Homer, the virtues of superior humans are noble descent, physical beauty, courage, and wisdom. Honour is a measure of virtue, and fame is virtue's reward. This heroic ideal of life is shown by courage in battle and in athletic competition during times of peace. To know the reason and cause of events is not the concern of people, but the concern of the gods. To Homer, people had a strong desire to be judged well by others. A good reputation within a tribe or village and public respect were essential.

Trojan War Illustrations on Vases

For many centuries after the Trojan War, vase painters interpreted the deeds narrated in the *Iliad*. The frieze (from a vase) on the opposite page is an example.

From the top left, clockwise: Over a hundred thousand Greeks led by Agamemnon, the king of Mycenae, arrived at Troy. Greeks and Trojans engaged in heated combat. After ten years of fighting, Agamemnon took advantage of his authority as commander of the Greeks and stole the slave Briseid from Achilles. Consequently, Achilles refused to fight. In the meantime, prompted by the intervention of the gods, the two armies clashed in an open field under the watchful eyes of Helen and Priam. Paris, the prince of Troy, wished to have a duel with a Greek. Menelaus accepted the challenge and was about to win but, due to the intervention of Aphrodite, a general battle ensued. The Greek heroes, Odysseus and Diomedes, seized a spy and stopped the threat of an attack by the Trojans. Patroclus, a friend of Achilles, put on Achilles' armour and defended the Greeks, but the Trojan hero Hector killed him and chased Menelaus away. In celebration of his victory, Hector wore the armour of Achilles. When Achilles got the news of the death of his friend, he brandished his weapons and, under the protection of Athena, defeated and killed Hector who was protected by Apollo. Priam gave Achilles expensive gifts in exchange for his son's body. After several encounters, Achilles also died by the hand of Paris, who struck him on his heel with an arrow guided by the hand of Apollo.

Finally, the Greeks succeeded in entering Troy by hiding in the belly of a large wooden horse. In the looting that followed, Polyxina, the youngest daughter of Priam, was killed on Achilles's tomb. Cassandra, the sister of Paris, was abducted by the Greeks from the temple of Athena together with her mother Hecuba and Andromache, Hector's wife. Menelaus was reunited with Helen, and the only member of the Trojan royal family who succeeded in escaping was Aeneas, who was later, according to legend, to found Rome.

The Excavation of the City of Troy

Many archaeologists, first and foremost Heinrich Schliemann in the last century, believed that they had found the site of Troy on a hill called Hissarlik in the northwestern corner of Turkey. There, archaeological excavations have brought to light seven layers of urban occupation which have been dated between 2700 and 1100 B.C. Although there is no certain evidence, numerous scholars have no doubt about this location. The Trojan War is not just a legend; it was an actual event that took place in approximately 1200 B.C.

Opposite page, centre illustration: In a Greek village, a poet of the 800s B.C. sings of the deeds of the Trojan War which took place four hundred years earlier.

The main episodes of the Trojan War, as illustrated on a vase.

43

A merchant arrives in a fortified city, carrying jars and other Carthaginian products.

A warrior armed with an oval shield of the Celtic type and a scimitar.

The Area of the Celts/Iberians

After 700 B.C., Celtic populations which had separated early from the main group in central Europe settled on the Spanish peninsula. They developed independently from the main group, although they kept some features of their original culture. The Celt-Iberians were mainly found in the northern, central, and western parts of the peninsula.

In the kingdom of Tartessus, Phoenician influence was seen in gold work, which made use of tiny gold nuggets. Shown here are two examples from the treasure of Carambolo, Seville.

THE IBERIANS

Phoenicians and Carthaginians

The decline of the Mycenaean civilization slowed commercial trade in the eastern Mediterranean. The Phoenicians, who inhabited a narrow strip of coastal land close to the mountains of Lebanon in the Near East, were quick to grasp the opportunity as it arose. In the three harbours of Tyre, Sidon, and Biblos, they developed great skills in sailing. The mountains of Lebanon provided large quantities of trees, the famous cedars of Lebanon, for the construction of ships, and the Phoenicians had sufficient knowledge to navigate by using the stars. Soon they gained dominion over the Mycenaean commercial area and pushed further to the west. Between the ninth and eighth centuries B.C., they founded the colony of Carthage on the North African coast. Carthage was to become much more important than the motherland, Tyre. It was to spread the Phoenician culture, which had become Carthaginian culture, throughout the western Mediterranean.

The Phoenicians Reach Spain

Even before 1000 B.C., Phoenicians from Tyre had established trade with southern Spain. Around 1100 B.C., they founded the important colony of Gabez on the Atlantic coast, not far from the Strait of Gibraltar. The first Phoenicians sought metal-bearing minerals in Spain and brought to the area various precious objects and tools to exchange, as the Carthaginians did later. Up to the Roman conquest in the third century B.C., the Phoenician and Carthaginian civilizations were to have a major influence, both culturally and artistically, on the development of the Iberian civilization.

Iberian Civilization

The first important nucleus of Iberian civilization developed in the valley of the Guadalquivir River and in the surrounding mountain areas. This region roughly corresponded to modern day Andalusia in southern Spain, where the Phoenicians founded the first of their European colonies, Gabez, on the Atlantic coast. In this area, the city-state of Tartessus was founded. The economy of the area was highly developed, and the fertile

Right: A Greek vase found in a burial site in the colony of Ampurias. Several rituals and burial customs of Greece were adopted by the Iberians.

Left: An iron scimitar. This type of sword was used by the Iberians.

Below: A gold headband from Javea.

"lady of Elche", an e, multi-coloured

Left: The pink coloured part of the map represents the area occupied by the Iberians. The southern and coastal regions were exposed to Greek and Carthaginian influence.

Top: A family brings offerings to a sanctuary. *Above:* This frieze with warriors depicts the military skills of the Iberians. It was painted on a vase of the third century B.C.

valley of the Guadalquivir River sustained bountiful agriculture with good cereal crops. Metal trade was also important.

The Iberians of the East

Around the end of the sixth century B.C., Tartessus lost its importance for reasons which are still unknown. Dominance shifted to towns on the Mediterranean coast of Spain, in the eastern region. This region was highly influenced by Greece, both in frequent trade and in the continuous presence of Greek ships in the harbours, even though it seems that the Greeks never established an important settlement in Spain. The Carthaginians had absorbed the Phoenician tradition. After founding an important colony in the strategic location of Ibiza in the Balearic Islands, they created other colonies, in particular on the southern Mediterranean coast, and maintained great influence over the Iberian Peninsula.

Recent archaeological excavations of the first Iberian villages have brought to light the presence of common characteristics in the different settlements. All of these settlements developed as groups of various buildings which were divided by roads. The houses were clustered together, made of fired bricks on the lower portion and unfired bricks on the upper portion. Following a tradition which had begun in the late Bronze Age, these settlements were always fortified and placed on hills or small plateaus, which were easy to defend because of the steep slopes.

Also in these locations, agriculture developed greatly, taking advantage of the introduction of irrigation techniques. Weaving and artisanship also began to develop, and currency was circulated. At first it was Greek currency, but later it became local, with Phoenician or Celtic inscriptions. One of the most important aspects of the contact between these areas and other populations of the Mediterranean was the introduction of writing. Through the centuries, the rule of the towns passed from the hands of kings to the hands of a local aristocracy, formed by the landowners, who also enjoyed the status of warriors. However, the core of the army was formed of free men who served as mercenaries. At first, these soldiers were used in local wars, but later, Iberian troops went to fight in Carthaginian and Roman armies.

THE ITALICS

Italics is the name for the peoples living in the Italian peninsula before Rome came to dominate the region. Only recently have these people been given an identity, after new discoveries about life during the Iron Age (between 1000 and 500 B.C.).

Phoenician and Greek Colonization

As happened in Spain, the two major Italian islands, Sardinia and Sicily, were also colonized by the Phoenicians (in the eighth and seventh centuries B.C.) and the Carthaginians (sixth century). The Carthaginians, who were interested in mineral and agricultural products, maintained their rule and influence over these areas until the first Punic War when they were defeated by Rome in 241 B.C. Greek influence came as Mycenaean ships visited the southern coast of Italy.

But the great Greek expansion took place in two phases. Between 771 and 675 B.C., a full scale agricultural colonization took place, prompted by the need for new land. On the other hand, between 675 and 550 B.C., the Greek colonies also engaged in considerable trade. After establishing the colonies, its products were exported to Greece in exchange for various artifacts. Southern Italy and most of Sicily became known as "greater Greece" because of the number of colonies that had been established there. At the same time, a unique culture developed, independent from the motherland. However, the cultural and artistic contributions of Greece to these Italian areas were enormous.

The Expansion of the Celts

After the Greek colonies in the south had grown strong and formed an independent existence from Greece, Celtic populations descended into Italy from the northern regions. The Romans called these people Gauls. The presence of the Gauls was to increase particularly in northern Italy between the fifth and fourth centuries and culminated with the assault on and burning of Rome in 390 B.C. In 225 B.C., Rome resumed its policy of conquest and regained all of the territories lost to the Gauls. The Gauls were vastly different from the Greeks. They were a pastoral nomadic people, organized into tribes, and had not developed true towns. They often undertook raiding wars in the Italian peninsula.

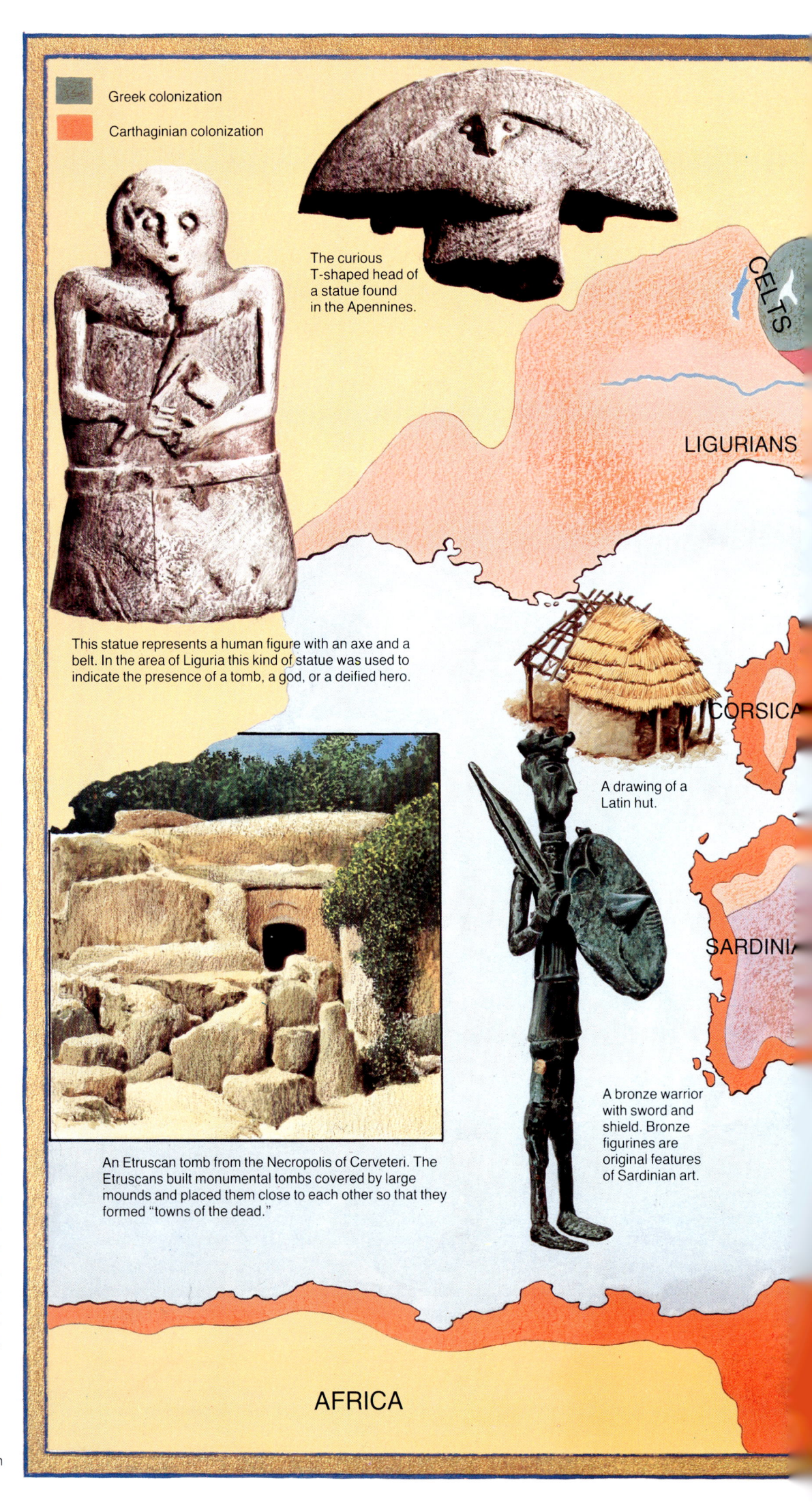

Shown here are the Italic peoples in the Iron Age, with examples of their art.

- Greek colonization
- Carthaginian colonization

The curious T-shaped head of a statue found in the Apennines.

This statue represents a human figure with an axe and a belt. In the area of Liguria this kind of statue was used to indicate the presence of a tomb, a god, or a deified hero.

A drawing of a Latin hut.

An Etruscan tomb from the Necropolis of Cerveteri. The Etruscans built monumental tombs covered by large mounds and placed them close to each other so that they formed "towns of the dead."

A bronze warrior with sword and shield. Bronze figurines are original features of Sardinian art.

CELTS
LIGURIANS
CORSICA
SARDINIA
AFRICA

A Name Lost in Legend

The Romans called the people of central and southern Italy Italics, and in time they were to clash with the Italics in the process of expanding their dominion. There is evidence of an Italic coalition against Rome. Later, the peoples of northern Italy who had lived in the Po Valley were also called Italics, except for the Celtic peoples.

Peoples of the Italian Peninsula

The Apulians (in Apulia) are divided into subgroups such as the Messapians and the Daunians. The Lucanians inhabited the region of the same name and extended farther toward Calabria, while the Brutians lived in the rest of Calabria, and the Sicilians lived on the part of Sicily which was not under the dominion of Greece or Carthage. The Latins inhabited southern Latium. Northern Latium and Tuscany were the lands of the Etruscans. Umbrians and Samnites inhabited the southern central part of the Apennines all the way to the Adriatic Sea, and the Picenians inhabited the Marche region. The Veneti lived in the area of the Po Delta, and the Ligurians inhabited the western part of the plain and Liguria. Later, a Celtic population was to settle between the territory of the Ligurians and Veneti. Still other peoples, such as the Rhaetians and Camunians, lived in the Alps.

The Camunians had been expressing themselves artistically for thousands of years, as the quantity of carved rocks that they left behind proves. Different languages of Indo-European origin were used on most of the peninsula, with the exception of the Ligurian, Sardinian, and Etruscan languages.

This great variety of populations had continuous relationships which enriched each of them. The history of all these people, with the exception of the Etruscans with whom the problem is more complicated, was influenced by encounters with the Carthaginians and Greeks. Undoubtedly, had it not been for these encounters, Italic populations would not have developed such a strong identity.

Their culture developed a system for writing, an important development which allowed the gathering and transmission of complex information. Variations in styles of art was a principal difference between the various peoples. The type of artistic expression gives a sense of the different ways in which these various groups handled influences from the outside, sometimes copying, sometimes changing, sometimes inventing new and original patterns with more imagination and sense of colour than the original models.

Left: Symbols of power in the Etruscan city-states included a stone axe, war trumpets, and *fasces* (bundles of sticks) carried by officials. At the bottom sits a magistrate with his sceptre. *Above:* The principal towns were centres around which political and economic life was organized. Each town controlled a different territory within the region.

Etruscan huts, a temple, a house, and another building.

THE ETRUSCANS—
POLITICAL STRUCTURE AND SOCIAL LIFE

In central and northern Italy, the rise of the Etruscans and of their cities marked a great change in political life, the economy, and the culture. The actions of the Etruscans, both in their homeland and in the territories of their later expansion, were dominated by two fundamental objectives—the control of the sites of metal production and rule over different commercial sea and land routes.

A population of merchants, builders, and engineers, the Etruscans never imposed a unified form of government on the regions which they controlled. On the contrary, they built a political structure based on city-states, which were similar to those created by the Greeks. The large towns together with villages and minor towns formed autonomous political entities. In the beginning, the leader of the city-state was a king. He was the political leader, the supreme judge, and the priest in one person. With the increase in trade, the power shifted from the hands of the king to the hands of the magistrates who were chosen from an elite group of noble and wealthy families. This government by the few is known as an oligarchy.

The Expansion of the Etruscan Civilization

Although independent, the city-states were allied to one another. It was an alliance mainly founded on religion and included regular meetings of priests from the various cities. Political and military alliances were much rarer and hardly ever included all of the towns.

Starting in the seventh century B.C., the Etruscans began to expand further southwards into the Italian peninsula, seeking contact with the Greek world. They gained permission to cross the land of the Latins and created several towns in Campania, the most important of which was Capua. In the following century, the Etruscans also expanded to the north and founded towns in the Po Valley. The most important of these towns was Felsina, today called Bologna. The plain of the Po River was well connected with routes that crossed the Alps to the lands of the Celts. The Adriatic Sea allowed contact with Greece.

Etruscan Society

The inhabitants of the Etruscan cities did not have equal rights, wealth, and quality of life. The countryside was divided into "lati-

The illustration above depicts social life in the house of an Etruscan noble. The guests are being entertained by a dancer and a musician. The insert depicts paintings from the tomb of the leopards (Tarquinii) which shows the festive atmosphere enjoyed by the Etruscans.

The Etruscan heartland (*inset*) and some of their main cities.

"fundia", which were vast stretches of land owned by a family group. The land was farmed by slaves or by people who rented the land. Some people also owned the land that they farmed. Families of nobles lived in the cities, and the magistrates and the king were chosen from among them. Aristocratic status was acquired either through merit gained in battle or through the accumulation of great wealth. Important merchant families also inhabited the Etruscan cities. Because of trade, nobles had a very high standard of living, higher than the status attained by the same type of people in the Greek towns and in Roman towns in Italy. They were surrounded by servants and by artisans. Free citizens would also put themselves under the protection of powerful noble patrons.

The number of artisans and small merchants gradually increased, but this group of people never gained sufficient strength to challenge the power of the aristocracy. From the frescoes found in the tombs, an image of the type of life led by wealthy Etruscans can be formed. They enjoyed social life. They would gather and spend time listening to music, dancing, dining and playing games.

Women

In Etruscan society, women had a good chance of participating in public life. The status of a woman, compared to a man, was more equal than elsewhere at that time. The mother, as well as the father, could give her name to her children. Women were considered to have powers of divination and healing, and some had strong political influence.

Agriculture and Engineering

Where conditions were favourable, the Etruscans developed agriculture, mainly through farming previously drained land. They also used complex irrigation systems, including reservoirs and underground channels.

The Etruscans were masters of metal-working, as is seen from these examples of their skill (inserts, right and left). Centre: Coppersmiths smelting copper ore in furnaces. Below: An example of Etruscan writing carved on a lead plaque.

THE ETRUSCANS—MERCHANTS, ARTISANS, GREAT ARTISTS, AND RELIGIOUS PEOPLE

A Population of Merchants

A great part of the wealth for which the Etruscans were famous, even among their contemporaries, was the result of their intense commercial activities. They were known as merchants and traders. They sold highly-prized metals throughout the Mediterranean, together with various artisan products which were often made in large quantities. Moreover, they resold products of Greek origin and Near Eastern origin which they obtained from their trade with the Greeks.

Trade was carried on by sea, and the Etruscans were very skilled sailors. They sailed both for trade and to raid various regions, looking for valuable booty. Piracy was a very common practice in the ancient Mediterranean. Due to Greek influence, navigation techniques were advanced, and sea travel brought Etruria to the peak of its cultural and political power. This is evident from the fact that around 600 B.C., the sea of western Italy began to be referred to as the Tyrrhenian Sea, from the name given to the Etruscans by the Greeks.

This tight network of communication, helped by the occasional "middle-men" activities of the Greeks, explains the extraordinary spread of Etruscan products. Goods produced in this northern Italian civilization reached Spain, northern Africa, Belgium, Germany, and southern Russia.

Above is a description of death according to the Etruscan religion. The pictures show a warrior killed in combat falling first into the power of the malevolent demon Tuchulcha, and then being led by Charun (Charon) into the next world.

Above: The burial of an Etruscan noble. The interior of the tomb is shown in the insert. *Right:* A soothsayer observes the entrails of an animal in order to predict the future. In the foreground is a bronze model of a sheep liver which was used to teach the art of divination (third or second century B.C.).

Etruscan Metallurgy

The Etruscans excelled in and were famous for their techniques of extracting minerals and metals. They worked with copper, iron, lead, tin, and silver. The techniques they used to extract the minerals were the same as those used in other parts of Europe. Close to their mines, which often had extensive tunnels, they built complexes of smelting furnaces to produce a great quantity of metal.

Language

The Etruscans spoke a language probably different from other Italic tongues. The only knowledge of it is from a few inscriptions which have been preserved. They were written using the Greek alphabet, but so far no one has succeeded in decoding the meaning of the words. There is a rough knowledge of the topics of these inscriptions (liturgical and ceremonial texts, religious formulas, and lists of names), but the structure of the language itself is still unknown.

Art

The first Etruscan people were greatly influenced by Greek and Near Eastern art. They studied the many objects brought back by merchants. This encounter with the Greeks prompted the great imitative and creative skills of the Etruscans. The Etruscans created original techniques in jewellery making. Their first paintings were also influenced by Near Eastern art. Good examples of these are the quantities of paintings that decorate tombs. For their rich colours and the liveliness of their scenes, Etruscan paintings are certainly one of the major artistic expressions of ancient times.

Religion

From the Greeks, the Etruscans adopted images of gods having human shapes. The Etruscan religion was based on sacred writings that the Etruscans believed to be the expression of supernatural beings. The sacred books of the Etruscans taught the interpretation of lightning and of the prophetic signs to be found in the entrails of sacrificed animals.

The Legend of Aeneas:
In the first century B.C., the Roman poet Virgil wrote *The Aeneid*. This epic poem tells the story of the Trojan hero, Aeneas, the son of Venus. Aeneas escaped from Troy when it was destroyed by the Greeks. After many misadventures, he landed in Italy at the mouth of the Tiber in a land ruled by King Latinus. Aeneas married Latinus's daughter, Lavinia, and founded a town of the same name. When the king died, Aeneas succeeded him.

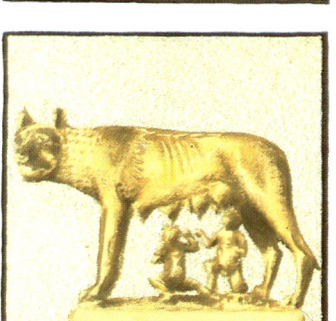

The Legend of the Founding of Rome:
After many generations, two babies descended from Aeneas, Romulus and Remus, were abandoned on the banks of the Tiber. A she-wolf reared the babies. When they grew up, the two brothers decided to found a city on the hills overlooking the Tiber, but they quarrelled and fought. Romulus killed Remus and founded the city of Rome, of which he became the first king.

Above: In Rome at the time of the Etruscan kings, an Etruscan magistrate supervises the construction of a new stone building. Latin huts of more ancient origin built with wood and clay can be seen on the left.

THE BIRTH OF ROME AND THE DECLINE OF THE ETRUSCANS

The Site of Rome

The Tiber River marked the boundary between Etruria and the territory of the Latins and was navigable in its lower reaches. Rome was founded on a site where seven hills were situated, close to the Tiber and not far from the Tiber's outlet into the Tyrrhenian Sea. The soil was fertile, vital saltworks were close by, and the seven hills formed a natural defence.

The First Kings of Rome

As early as the tenth century B.C., several villages existed on the seven hills, and Rome resulted from the merging of these villages. Within a very short time, Rome was bigger than the other towns and became the main commercial centre of the region. Rome was first ruled by kings. For the Latins, a king did not merely have economic or political power. He issued justice by deciding right or wrong and decreed what should be done to conform to the will of the gods. From the beginning of the monarchy, the influence of the Etruscans on Rome was very strong. Etruscans, Greeks, and Carthaginians would gather to trade at the Forum Boarium close to the river, but the Etruscans were responsible for major works such as the drainage of the forum—an area that was swampy and uninhabitable—and the construction of the great sewage system called the *cloaca maxima*. It is probable that in this

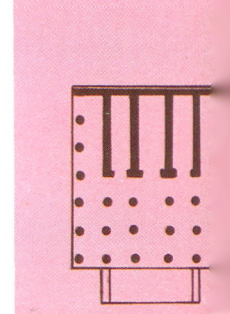

The Great Etruscan Monument in Rome

Shown (*right*) is the ground plan and replica of the temple of Jupiter Capitolium, which was built by the Etruscans on the Campidolium in 509 B.C. This is the largest of all known Etruscan temples. Some specific characteristics of the Etruscan temples are that the columns did not run all around the temple (as in Greek temples) and that the rear wall was solid. The interior is divided into three sections or chambers. The Etruscan temples had beams and architraves made of wood, sometimes covered with terra-cotta tiles.

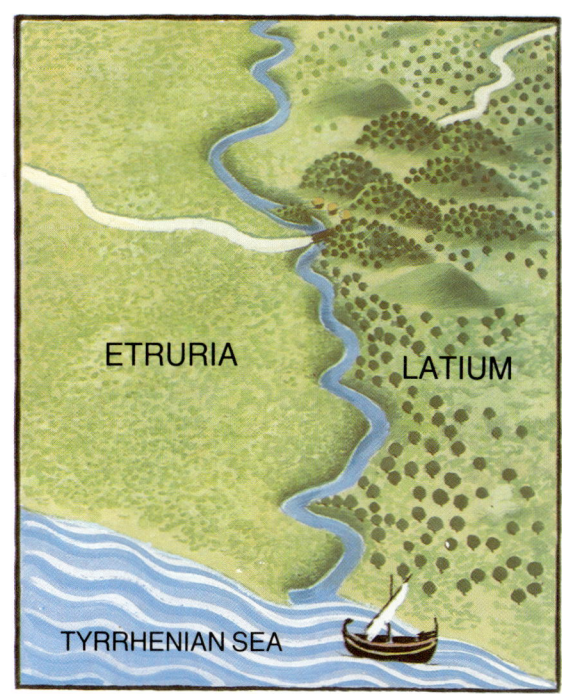

Above: The map shows the location where Rome was to be built, at the ford of the Tiber. Below are the seven hills of Rome. The walls of Servius Tullius are highlighted in blue.

The Period of the Etruscan Kings in Rome

The first Etruscan king was Tarquinius Priscus, who ruled between 616 and 579 B.C. He was followed by other Etruscan kings— Servius Tullius, whose Etruscan name was Mastarna, and by the last Etruscan king, Tarquinius Superbus. During the time of the Etruscan government, the city of Rome was greatly developed. It was surrounded by powerful defensive walls made of porous rock called tufa. The walls partially stand today. The institutions of the town remained Latin, but a certain Etruscan influence, especially in clothing and art, was visible. In particular, Etruscan religious influence was to last for a long time. In addition to Etruscan, the Romans spoke a language from which Latin was to develop in later times.

The Decline of Etruscan Power

From about 600 B.C., the Etruscan world experienced a political and military crisis, triggered by the hostility of the Latins, the Greeks to the south, and later by the pressure of the Celts from the north. In the city of Rome, the Latin aristocracy rose against the last Etruscan king and forced him out, changing the system of government into a republic. A group of Latin towns defeated the Etruscans, forcing them to abandon conquered territory.

To the south, the tension with towns of Greek origin and especially the rivalry between the Etruscans and the towns of Cuma and Syracuse gradually grew. It finally broke out in a series of armed confrontations which ended in a victory for the Greeks. At sea, the Etruscan fleet was gradually reduced by the Greek and Carthaginian fleets, but the conquest of the Etruscan city-state territories was mainly the work of the Romans. In the fourth and the third centuries B.C., Celtic tribes from Gaul seized northern Italy, blocking the Alpine routes which were essential to Etruscan commerce. The decline of the Etruscans would end in the conquest of Etruria by Rome.

Iron extraction was done in small kilns or furnaces. Bellows were necessary to raise the temperature inside the furnace. At the end of the process, the furnaces were cracked open, and the mass of melted iron was extracted and later worked on an anvil. The insert illustrates how the furnace was loaded. A pit in the ground was filled with green branches, and then the iron ore was alternated with layers of charcoal.

Below: Various bronze and iron objects found at Hallstatt.

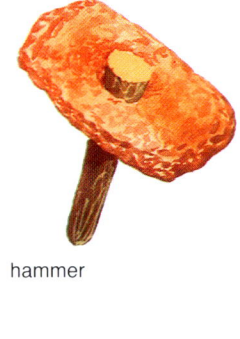

pick axe

bucket

scythe

hammer

THE IRON AGE BEGINS

The Salt Industry

From the Mediterranean, the area of city states and of advanced civilizations which are still famous today, we turn to temperate Europe north and west of the Alps. An example of what took place here at the end of the Bronze Age and at the beginning of the Iron Age can be found at Hallstatt, a village in the Austrian Alps along the Danube.

A very important activity had developed in the territories included in what is today Austria and Germany. It was the extraction of rock salt from mines. Salt was not obtained from saltworks by the sea (by evaporating water enclosed in small lagoons) but was instead taken from rock and then placed in artificial pools to be purified. The importance of salt had been constantly growing. It was beginning to be used for both preserving and cooking meat and vegetables.

Archaeological excavations at Hallstatt have uncovered knowledge of the process of the extraction of this important mineral. Rock salt was mined in tunnels carved almost 350 metres into the heart of the mountain, using pick axes and bronze axes, wooden shovels, and leather containers reinforced with wooden frames. Also common were knapsacks and baskets made by weaving ropes and vegetable fibres. The miners wore clothing made of dark wool which was probably patterned with colourful vegetable dyes. Their footwear consisted of leather moccasins, and they wore goatskin hats.

A Plus for Archaeologists

A plus-factor of salt is that it stops the decomposition of vegetable matter and of any organic matter. Therefore, ancient tools and clothing used in the production of salt have survived intact to the present day.

Europe Learns Iron-working

After 1000 B.C., the miners in Hallstatt, who were excellent bronze workers, also learned how to work iron. Iron objects made by hammering, without applying heat, have been found in places all over Europe, but the first proof of iron smelting dates from the first millennium B.C. In Greece, the first iron objects appeared in the eleventh century B.C. while in Romania and Yugoslavia, they mainly appeared in the ninth and eighth centuries B.C. The artisans of the Mediterranean world had learned how to work iron from the Greeks and the Etruscans. Knowledge of these techniques probably reached southern Germany and

The extraction of salt from the mines of Hallstatt in Austria at the beginning of the first millennium B.C. Salt was obtained by dissolving the mineral in large pools and then letting the water evaporate. *Insert:* Workers inside a salt mine.

saw — hub of a wheel — dagger — spear point

Austria through northern Italy and through the Alps. These regions were the heart of the Hallstatt iron culture of the eighth century B.C.

The Advantages of Iron

One of the first advantages of iron was in the production of better weapons, with sharper points and blades. After weapons, pliers, axes, and tools for farming were produced. Generally, iron became the favourite metal for all the tools used for craft work and transportation because it was more resistant to shock, and it was longer lasting. Decorative items for clothing, jewellery, and vessels continued to be made of copper and bronze because of the beauty of these metals. Iron tools became widely used in woodworking, allowing more precise cutting and finishing of wood.

The Emergence of Recorded Peoples

Between the Bronze Age and the Iron Age, archaeological documentation in Europe is abundant. The peoples referred to in the Greek and Roman texts started to emerge with their own ethnic identities. The Mediterranean area was home to the Etruscans, the Italics, the Iberians, and above all, the Greeks. The Illyrians emerged in Yugoslavia. Across the Alps and in central Europe, the Celtic populations gradually acquired their identity. The Scythians inhabited the eastern Steppes, while the Slavic peoples lived in the wooded areas of eastern Europe.

Techniques and Problems in the Production of Iron

Iron-bearing minerals are much more commonly found than the minerals bearing copper and tin, which were necessary to produce bronze. In northern Europe, iron ore is common and could be found in swamps and peat bogs in the form of little nodules. However, due to difficulty in processing, the mineral had been long left unused. Iron melts at approximately 1,535°C, and this temperature could not be reached until the fourteenth century B.C. after the invention of bellows in Europe. A kind of iron could be directly obtained from the mineral by heating it to approximately 800-900°C. The product was a metal that could be worked but was not very resilient.

In order to obtain better results, some technical improvements were necessary. It was best that the mineral be heated to around 1,100°C, a temperature which could be obtained by the people who knew how to work copper. Secondly, some carbon had to be added, thus transforming iron into steel, a harder and more resilient metal. This could be done by using coal as fuel and by allowing only a little air into the furnace. The metal had to be quickly cooled and then tempered, which means it had to be heated and cooled again.

THE WARRIORS OF HALLSTATT

The Birth of a Warlike Aristocracy

Between the eighth and sixth centuries B.C., a powerful military class guided by new leaders ruled the world of Hallstatt. The Celtic people of Hallstatt did not have a unified government. Instead, there were independent agricultural groups, held together by a social organization and headed by groups of warriors, leaders, or princes. In time, this led to the establishment of dynasties. This local aristocracy based its power on two main factors. First, they owned large herds of sheep and cattle. Second, they acquired food and other goods which passed or were exchanged through their territory.

The Fortifications

Common people lived in villages in small scattered settlements, but each tribe had fortified defences where they could seek shelter in case of danger. The nobles had a separate residence. They lived in fortified palaces in the hills or on the plain. These fortified dwellings were useful to defend wealth and cattle in case of danger, but they also functioned as large commercial centres. They were located between southern and northern Europe, forming trade routes along which travelled large wagons with four iron-spoked wheels.

Control of commercial traffic became increasingly important when, due to the development of Greek and Etruscan civilizations along the coast of the Mediterranean, a new cultural source came into being near temperate Europe. As a result, trade intensified, renewing ancient routes and creating new ones.

In the sixth century, trade was facilitated by the foundation of Massilia, located at the mouth of the Rhone River. The Rhone acted as a long corridor which was easily travelled from the Alpine region to the sea. Trade was also increased by the creation of the towns of Adria and Spina on the northern coast of the Adriatic Sea. These towns were easily reached through the Alpine passes. The Hallstatt people received tin from Great Britain, copper from the Alps, gold from the Rhine region and Bohemia, and amber, furs, and slaves from the Baltic region. From the south, it received elegant fabrics, amphoras, ceramics, vessels such as pitchers, cups, horns, strainers, and buckets, and wine – which was the most important food item imported by the people living in northern Europe. These goods and their merchants brought with them new customs and new ways of thinking and of living.

Life and Death of the Warriors

The privileged position reserved for warriors and leaders was particularly expressed in the funeral rites. For example, a dead prince was first laid in state. Afterwards, his body was either buried or carried to a cremation site (both customs were in use) on a ritual wagon richly decorated with metal ornaments. The burial site was built with stones or wood and covered by a dirt mound. Numerous offerings of food (usually a quarter of a pig) and a knife (to be used in the feast that was to take place in the kingdom of the dead) were placed beside the body. A multitude of other artifacts were also buried with the dead. Certainly, local products were not enough for the requirements of the aristocracy. Products from as far away as Etruria and Greece were greatly sought after. Wine, a Mediterranean product, was a central element of the feasts of this society.

The First Celts

Many scholars consider Hallstatt to be one of the points of origin of the Celtic people. The Celts were to become, within a short time, a large population with its own culture and way of life that was to spread over most of Europe. Their modern descendants, the Irish, Scots, Welsh, and Bretons, were later pushed to the western edges of the European continent.

Above: An illustration of a hut at Heuneburg.

Opposite page: The Hallstatt type of fortification at Heuneburg, on the Danube, was characterized by having walls made of brick. This was a Mediterranean feature resulting from Greek influence. *Insert:* Brickmakers at work, using clay and straw.

Below: The main trade routes between central Europe and the Mediterranean world. The pink area indicates the extent of the Hallstatt culture.

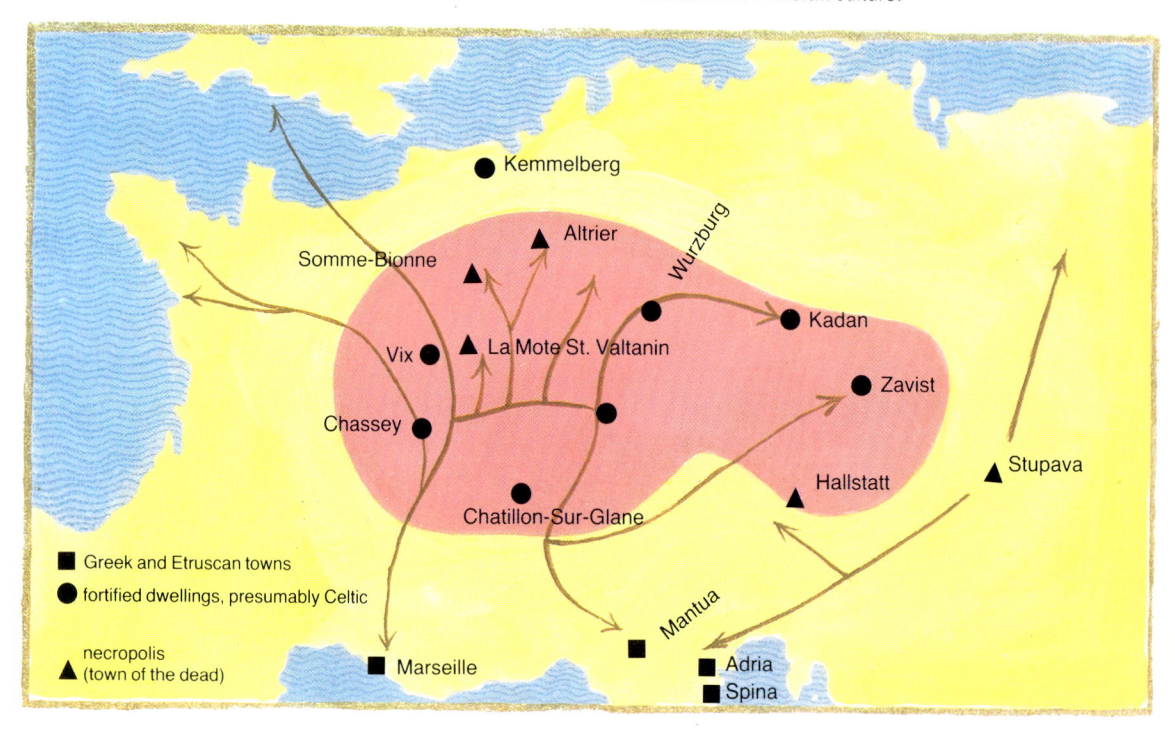

Below: Inside the tomb of a Hallstatt prince in Hochdorf, Germany, with the ritual wagon.

57

Above: The situla or bronze vessel found at Vace in Slovenia, famous for the beauty of its decoration.

Chariot racing was one of the favourite sports of the aristocratic society of the Veneti.

The decorative bands of the Vace vessel show, from top to bottom: a chariot race, a wine ceremony, what looks like a boxing match, and an animal frieze.

The map shows the area in which the art of situlae-making was practised.

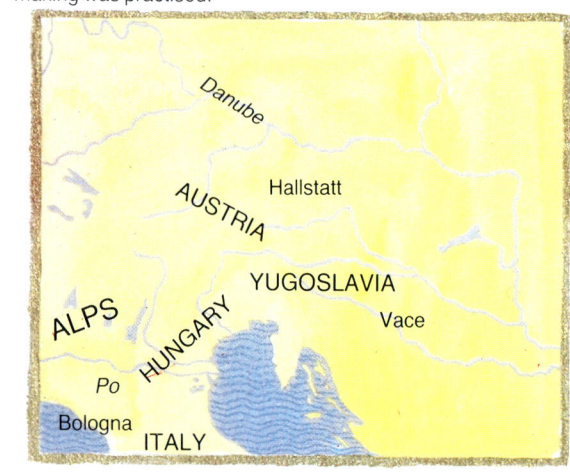

A chariot racer shows a trophy he has just won.

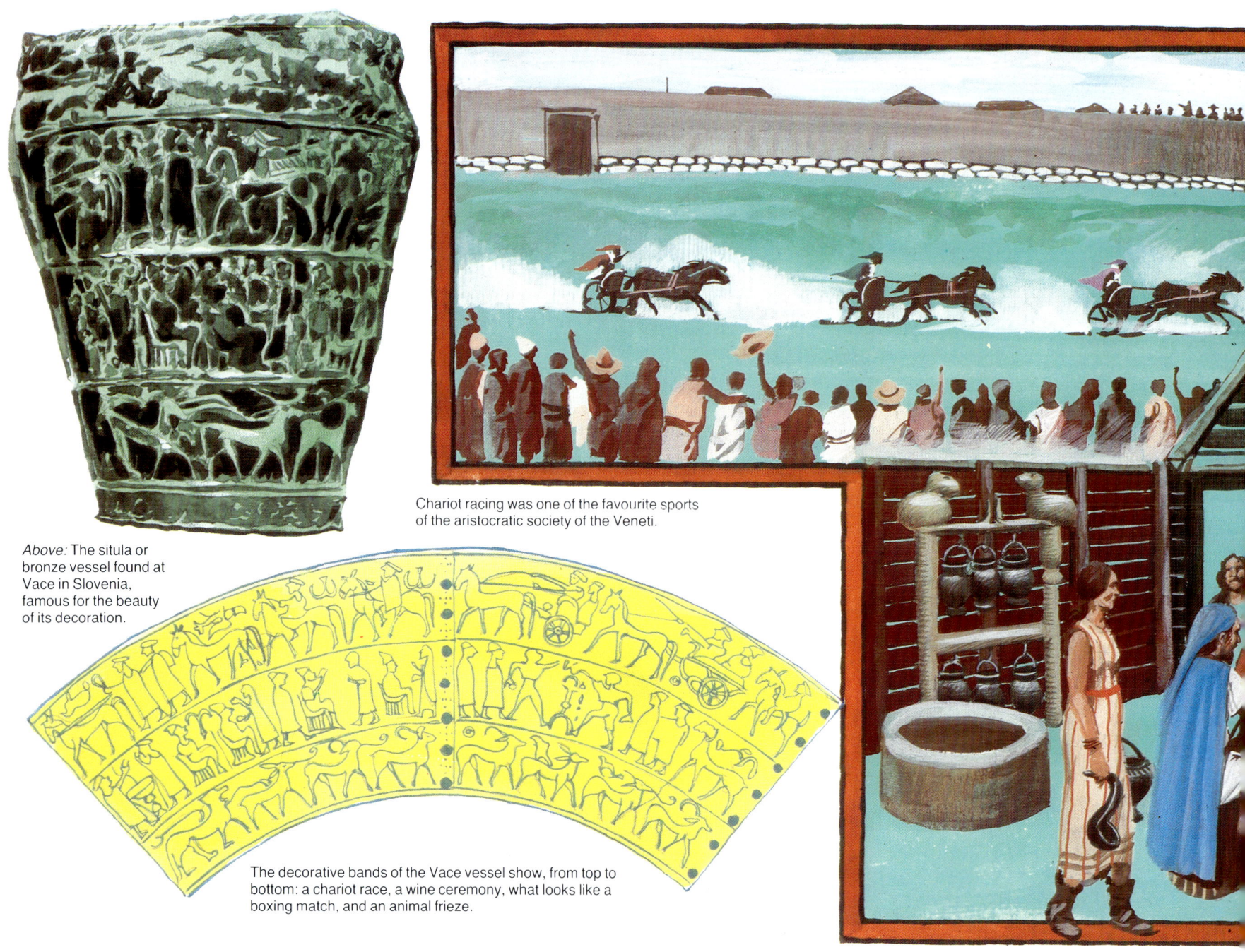

A REFINED BUT WARLIKE WORLD

A Wealthy and Art-loving Society

At the beginning of the Iron Age, a refined civilization developed close to the Hallstatt world. It was east of the Danube in what is now Slovenia (Yugoslavia) and in the region around Venice (Italy), between the Alps to the Adriatic Sea, which also included the easternmost section of the Po Valley. These people, the Veneti, produced works of art of great value such as *situlae*, distinctive bronze vessels with lids.

Even in the Iron Age, more precious metals continued to be preferred for the manufacture of many different things, especially objects of art. The art of the Veneti reveals a culturally sophisticated people and provides detailed information about their lives. Embossed on the situlae are important events in the history of the first Veneti and of the inhabitants of Slovenia and southern Austria. These peoples absorbed numerous influences. The lands which they inhabited were to become the hub for people from the south, the north, the east, and the west. The first Veneti (whose territory bordered the Etruscans to the south and the first Celtic populations to the northeast) had links to Greece and to the Aegean world across the Adriatic Sea. They gained great advantage from this strategic position.

Daily Life

The decorations on the situlae present an overall view of the social life of the time. The vessels were decorated in parallel bands, some of which were ornamental and bore plant and animal patterns, while others were similar to modern cartoons. Scenes of war and daily life are represented in horizontal bands and tell a vivid story of the times.

Although the illustrations showed mytholo-

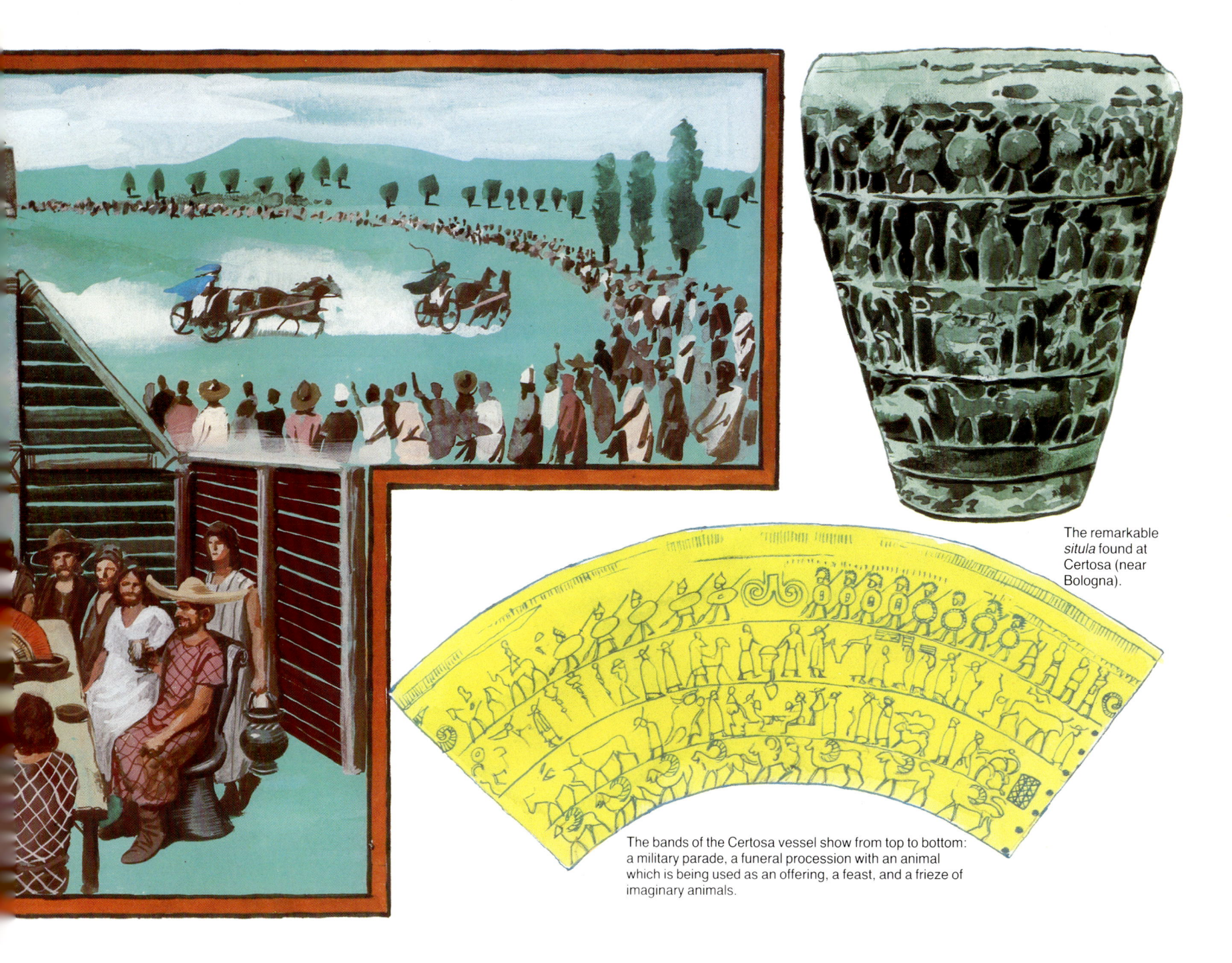

The remarkable *situla* found at Certosa (near Bologna).

The bands of the Certosa vessel show from top to bottom: a military parade, a funeral procession with an animal which is being used as an offering, a feast, and a frieze of imaginary animals.

gical events, the way of life they describe is undoubtedly that of the Veneti and Celtic/Venetian aristocracy of the sixth century B.C. It was a male-dominated, warlike aristocracy. Women were confined to the home. Women were represented participating in work such as spinning and weaving, for example. Men were the warlike aristocrats that Homer described. This society was filled with the idea of the "heroic" life.

One of the themes most frequently represented in situlae decoration is the feast. Various male figures, often holding sceptres or flutes, are comfortably lying around, while women or servants offer them drinks. Wine drinking was common. The mixing, filtering, and pouring of wine are often depicted.

Games and War

Games were among the most important features of social life during these times. Depicted on the situlae are boxing matches, chariot races, and other races of various kinds together with religious festivities. Sacrifices, processions, and military parades also decorate the situlae. The latter are of special interest because they document an important change in the techniques of war. Military clashes were no longer entirely dependent on the expert skills of noble cavalrymen, but were carried out by arranging groups of infantry in the field who would confront the enemy in formations. This strategy required continuous training, to perfect marching in ranks to confront the enemy. The infantry carried heavy weapons. Each man went to battle with a helmet, a large spear, and an oval or round shield.

The Situlae

Situlae are vessels rather like pails. They are shaped like truncated cones, 20 to 25 centimetres high, with a narrowed bottom, a rounded shoulder, a wide mouth with a short rim, and a flat lid. These vessels developed from urns which for centuries had been used to hold the ashes of the dead. They were made of bronze and were decorated with a series of scenes embossed or engraved on several horizontal bands. The oldest situlae date back to the seventh century B.C., and the most recent date from the fifth century B.C.

Above: A Scythian campsite in the steppes of Russia. The wagons had very large wheels. Many furnishings like the table depicted in the illustration could be disassembled to ensure rapid moves from camp to camp. The insets highlight some aspects of daily life: the skinning of an animal, the dress of a warrior, and the start of the day's hunt, with a man mounting his horse (without stirrups).

Europe and the peoples of the steppes

THE SCYTHIANS

The Life of the Scythians

The Scythians were a people who lived in what is now Russia, in the regions which surround the Caspian and Black seas. The Scythians had a close relationship with the Greek colonies on the Black Sea and established a flourishing commerce. The Greeks were ready to satisfy the needs of this "barbarian" population who offered hides, wood, wheat, and slaves in exchange for wine and artisan crafts. Obviously, the Greek colonizers had knowledge of the populations of the inland regions with whom they traded, and the ancient writers left interesting accounts of them.

From these accounts, it is known that the territory between the mouths of the Danube and the Don rivers was called Scythia and was inhabited by tribes with different names. Among these, the Scythians dominated. They spoke an Indo-European language, and their physical features were similar to those of the Europeans. Some of them were skilled farmers who lived in efficient farming villages. Some of their fortified dwellings have been found. But most Scythians were nomads. They did not cultivate the land, but instead led their herds of grazing animals from pasture to pasture. The necessity of leading and increasing their herds determined their way of life. They lived in tents made of skins and moved in large wagons containing all of their belongings.

The Scythians knew the techniques of ironworking and built fortresses which were surrounded by defensive walls. The clothing of the Scythians included large, soft hats which completely covered the head, short jackets, belts, trousers, and leather boots.

An Equestrian People

The Scythians were very skilled riders. They rode with the aid of a blanket only. They fastened their weapons to their backs, carrying a bow, a short sword, a battle-axe, and a light spear. Particularly well known and feared were the archers who were able to use their bows and arrows very efficiently on horseback. The Scythians were also admired for their ability to move quickly on their horses. In battle, they

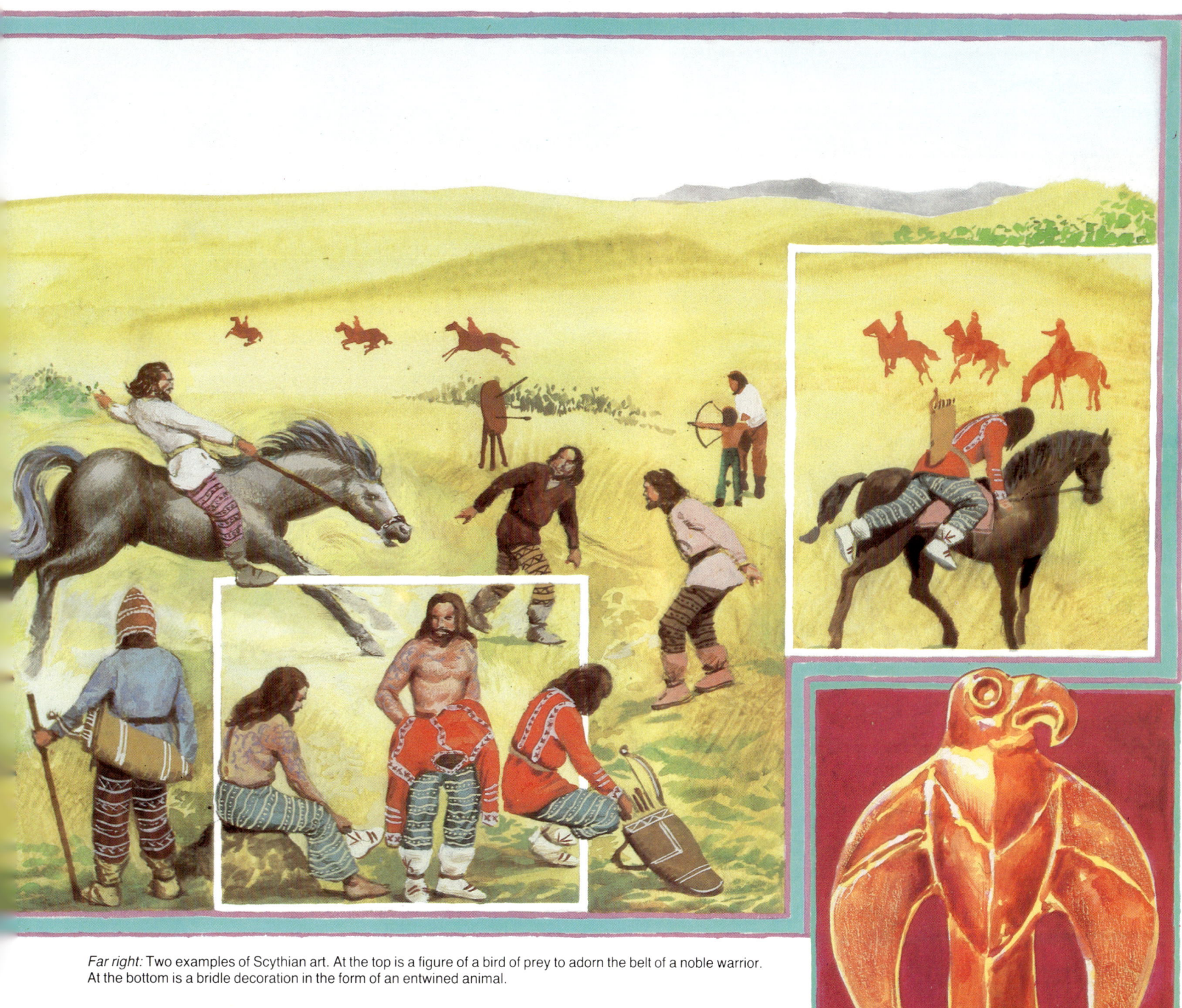

Far right: Two examples of Scythian art. At the top is a figure of a bird of prey to adorn the belt of a noble warrior. At the bottom is a bridle decoration in the form of an entwined animal.

could not be captured unless they decided to engage in close battle with the enemy.

The Scythians were ruled by a king with absolute power. The king lived in a large fortress, around which were royal tombs, some still visible today. Each horseman could obtain fame and honour through individual heroic actions. The power of the noble warriors was expressed in the splendour of the funerals. These are recounted by the historian Herodotus and the other Greek observers and confirmed by the numerous tombs that have been found. The leader was placed in a central chamber surrounded by sacrificial victims – his servants and concubines. Around the chamber, large numbers of sacrificial horses were placed in an orderly pattern. Many precious objects and gold cups filled the chamber which was covered by a mound.

Art and Gold Objects

The objects that have been found by archaeologists indicate that the Scythians loved to be surrounded by colourful, beautiful artifacts. These were made of various materials. Leather and felt were commonly used, overlaid with patterns in spiral designs and elaborate flourishes. Bone, bronze, and gold were also used for ornamentation. Cases, carpets, saddle blankets, harnesses, horses, wagons, and tents were decorated. The Scythians were famous for their extensive use of gold and for their skills at working it.

THE CELTS

From the fifth century B.C., there are increasingly numerous references to the Celtic peoples in the works of ancient writers.

The Crisis of the Aristocracy of Hallstatt

The Hallstatt culture, begun by the Celtic people, was a heroic society. It was ruled by a warlike aristocracy in central Europe. At the end of the sixth century B.C. it faced a crisis. The large fortified dwellings were destroyed or abandoned, and the number of elaborate tombs decreased. The people of nobility could not survive changes in warfare which increased the power of the common people. A change in climate may have also contributed to the decline of the Hallstatt culture. Finally, the increasing contacts with the Mediterranean civilizations undermined the old Celtic civilization.

The New Celtic World

The Celtic culture which replaced the aristocracy of Hallstatt is called the La Tène culture. La Tène is a site along the Swiss lake of Neuchatel where the first evidence of the Celtic peoples was found and studied. The La Tène culture was that of late Iron Age Celts who spread across Europe reaching the borders of the Mediterranean civilizations (Greeks, Etruscans, and Carthaginians). Instead of a uniform Celtic civilization, numerous regional features were intermixed with previous civilizations. The Celts did not unite politically, and they spoke different dialects. But they had a common ethnic origin and an art that was unique to them.

Above: A harness piece with red enamel, Britain, first century B.C.

Part of a trumpet in the shape of a boar's head. In the background is a war trumpet with an animal's head, as represented in the famous Gundestrup cauldron, Denmark, second century B.C.

Bronze helmet with horns from the Thames region of England 30 to 10 B.C.

Wheeled bronze ritual object with a hunting scene, Merida, Spain, around 100 B.C.

Right: A coin from southern Gaul.

Shown is the gradual creation of the Celtic civilization—the world of Hallstatt, then the culture of La Tène, and finally development in other parts of Europe. On the map are some important archaeological finds and art forms of the Celts.

During the Christian Era (A.D.), Celtic peoples were pushed to the northwestern fringes of Europe.

Gold necklace from the late Celtic Age, Snettisham, Norfolk, England.

Right: An iron clasp, used to fasten the ends of a garment, France.

This bronze ornament was part of a cremation burial, southern Germany.

HALLSTATT

Terra-cotta vases from a French tomb of the La Tène period.

LA TÈNE

GERMANS

This figurine of a horseman was part of a chariot used in seventh century B.C., Austria.

A rectangular house, typical of temperate Europe in Celtic times.

Right: Horse's bit from Galway, Ireland.

SCYTHIANS

Left: A boar which decorated a Celtic helmet, Hungary, first century B.C.

HALLSTATT in Austria was the centre of a Celtic civilization which flourished at the gateway of temperate Europe in the eighth to sixth centuries B.C. **LA TÈNE** in Switzerland on the lake of Neuchatel gave its name to the later Iron Age Celtic culture.

HALLSTATT

LA TÈNE

RHAETIANS

VENETI

GAETAE

BLACK SEA

Left: An iron helmet decorated with a bird of prey with bronze wings. It was found in the tomb of a prince at Ciumestia in Romania, third century B.C.

URIANS

ETRUSCANS

ILLYRIANS

THRACIANS

LATINS

Below: A coin of the Redones, a Celtic tribe of northwestern Gaul (France)

GREEKS

Right: A large bronze vase found in the Celtic tomb of the "Lady of Vix" in France. It was made in Greece and was perhaps produced specially for export.

This Celtic/Italic helmet with ear and neck guards is made of bronze.

- Core of the Celtic territory until the fifth century B.C.
- Influence of Celtic culture, as evident in the fifth century B.C.
- Spread of Celtic tribes from the end of the fifth century B.C.
- Celt-Iberians: linguistic and cultural influence from central Europe before the sixth century B.C.

63

La Tène art took inspiration from Greek and Etruscan models. Celtic art was enriched by the contact with Italics and Greeks. *Right:* A veteran warrior who has come back to his village on the shores of a Swiss lake describes to an artisan a pattern which he saw in Italy.

Far left: A sword with a handle in a human shape (Switzerland). *Left:* A decorated scabbard found in Marna in France, but possibly produced in a Danube workshop (third century B.C.). Animal and plant patterns overlap in an intricate design. This design is uniquely Celtic.

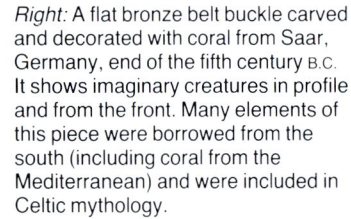

Right: A flat bronze belt buckle carved and decorated with coral from Saar, Germany, end of the fifth century B.C. It shows imaginary creatures in profile and from the front. Many elements of this piece were borrowed from the south (including coral from the Mediterranean) and were included in Celtic mythology.

EUROPE OF THE CELTS— THE CIVILIZATION OF LA TÈNE

Rural Communities Changing the Landscape

The new Celtic civilization which developed around the middle of the first millennium B.C., opening a new stage in the Iron Age, was essentially rural. The Celtic people had shown great skill in combining agriculture and animal rearing. Their skills in farming were enhanced by the spread of iron tools.

The Celts of the La Tène period already possessed tools of a kind which, little changed, were to be used in European agriculture up to the last century, and they introduced such tools everywhere they settled. The Celts expanded farming and colonized temperate Europe. They changed the European landscape by dividing it into farmland, pastures, and forested areas. The types of dwellings also corresponded to the new rural landscape. The Celts of La Tène did not live in large villages or in fortified towns. They were scattered in numerous small villages. Most likely, each territory was divided, and land given to families according to need.

There is evidence of a social hierarchy in village life. In the fifth century B.C., the leaders of the communities were buried with their swords. The wealthiest men were often buried with a spear and javelin. The women wore numerous ornaments which indicated their social status. Often they wore neck collars and ankle bracelets. Social position was probably inherited, as was the land. The continuity of the type of clothing and burials is proof of social stability in Celtic culture.

The endless changes in nature, as often seen in the play of light in the woods, must have inspired Celtic artists (as shown, *left*). In such natural phenomena, the Celts saw mysterious presences.

An Example of Embellishment on a Greek Design

This drawing shows detail on a Celtic bronze necklace. The artist was inspired by a classic Greek decoration in the form of foliage, which was entwined around the necklace. By rotating the decoration, the artist created two faces which were not part of the original decoration. This reveals a typical pattern of Celtic art, that of a god drawn by using patterns of leaves with two berries of mistletoe, a plant held sacred.

Decorations on a necklace from the end of the fourth century, beginning of the third century B.C. (Marna, France).

Above: The end of the bronze fibula (clasp) of Parsberg (Germany, end of the fifth century B.C.). It is in the shape of a head, only 15 mm high. This tiny object shows how Celtic artists could take a theme and rework it into a complex of geometric shapes, using space, light, and shade.

Everyday Objects

One of the elements which gave unity and cohesion to the Celtic population, which was scattered between Britain and the Black Sea, was the development of a new art style. The Celts left no monumental art. Only objects for practical use, both in war and peace, have been found. The artistic genius of the Celts was expressed in the decorations of the surfaces of these objects, obtained either through the use of simple lines or by means of relief of varying depth on metal, stone, and possibly wood.

At the end of the fifth century B.C., a style matured which was to appear throughout the Celtic world within a short time. The new style was called curvilinear because it was based on curved lines taken from observations of nature. Objects decorated with these patterns were found throughout the Celtic world. Some of these patterns were inspired by designs from Greek art. In the beginning, the influence of Greece and Etruria was probably very strong, but the art of the Celts gradually became original.

The most characteristic aspect of Celtic art was its refusal to create an image in a realistic form as the classic artists of the Mediterranean world had done. The Celts preferred stylized, constantly changing images. This art probably did not have a ritual meaning, but it did attempt to draw people closer to understanding the mysteries hidden beneath everyday reality.

Illustration of a warrior with a horn, based on a bas-relief found in the Alps, 450-350 B.C.

This funerary stele showing a Celtic war chariot and two warriors was found in Padua, Italy.

Above: Raiding was one of the methods by which young Celts acquired the wealth needed for importance and social prestige in their homeland.

WARS AND CONQUESTS OF THE CELTS

Causes of Military Expansion

From the fourth century B.C., the Celtic presence in southern and eastern Europe became threatening. The reasons for this pressure, which lasted over two centuries, are found in the structure of the rural Celtic society. The density of the rural population limited the quantity of available resources. Land was probably passed down from generation to generation within each family, but with each new generation it gradually became insufficient to sustain all of the male heirs. The people who did not own land lost most of their social prestige. If they wanted to maintain their prestige, they had to accumulate some other kind of wealth. The young Celts possessed an important and valued virtue, their fighting skills, which they utilized in various ways. They went on colonizing expeditions to conquer new territories, gathered in bands to raid and rob Mediterranean settlements, or served as mercenaries in the armies of other peoples.

The Expansion in Italy

The first land to attract the Celts was Italy. Around 400 B.C., numerous small bands of warriors came in search of plunder and booty in the Po Valley, which was mostly under the rule of the Etruscans. In successive raids, the Celts succeeded in defeating the Etruscans.

Considerable numbers of Celts settled in the Po Valley without entering the territory of the Veneti. They pushed south along the backbone of the Italian peninsula and along the Adriatic coast until they occupied an area which brought them in direct contact with the Greeks in southern Italy and Greece. Other bands raided Rome and reached the southernmost region of Apulia. In 369 B.C., Dionysius, king of Syracuse in Sicily, hired Celts to serve as mercenaries in Sicily. They were sent to fight in Greece and later were employed by the Sicilian King Agathocles in North Africa. The expansion of the Celts in Italy was stopped by the Romans. With the help of several Italic tribes, the Romans checked the raiders. Later, in a series of wars, they forced the Celts out of the Etruscan territories.

Thereafter, the Celts were forced to mo

Left: A stone statue of a warrior in armour (southern France).

Below: An illustration of a surprise attack on an Italic village by Celtic raiders.

Above: A Gallic warrior with weapons, from the third century B.C.

War Techniques of the Celts

The success of the military campaigns of the Celts was based on the use of special techniques, which had a frightening and surprising effect on the enemy. The infantry was used in the assault, together with the cavalry and two-wheeled war chariots, which appeared at the end of the fifth century. The warriors attacked the enemy in their chariots at full speed, firing arrows, and blowing fierce blasts on their horns. Then they dismounted from their chariots and faced the enemy in hand-to-hand combat. The Celts also trained their horses to perform manoeuvres at high speed. For example, the horses could be stopped suddenly or turned abruptly. The main body of the army fought on foot. The Celts used siege ladders to scale the walls of besieged fortifications. They surrounded defensive trenches and hurled rocks upon the enemy. When under attack, the Celts used their chariots to form defensive barriers.

further to the north until they were limited to the Po Valley. They remained there until their territory became, in 82 B.C., the Roman province of Cisalpine Gaul.

In the Balkans

Another area which looked promising to the Celts was the Balkans because of the internal fighting in the Hellenistic world after the death of Alexander the Great. In the fourth century B.C., the Celts had already pushed into Illyria and Pannonia (today parts of Hungary and Yugoslavia), where they came into direct contact with Scythians, Dacians, and Greeks. But only in the third century did the presence of the Celts in the Balkans become intense and destructive. The kingdom of the Thracians was swept by Celtic raids, and several Celtic tribes succeeded in settling in Illyria. In 279 B.C., they devastated Macedonia and penetrated into Greece. Some groups crossed the Bosphorus Straits and reached Asia Minor. However, although seriously weakened by looting and raiding, the Greeks forced the invaders back.

The Celts in Britain and Effects of the Expansion

These movements produced various effects. First of all, they caused the spread of the new Celtic art and culture. In the third century, the art of La Tène extended as far as the Danube. To the north, the Celts reached Britain. Their expansion, which ended in the third century B.C., created a Celtic population, and a cultural tradition in the British Isles which has survived into modern times. The Gaelic spoken in Ireland, for example, is a Celtic language.

Above: The cult of human skulls was much more ancient than the Celts, but they incorporated it into their religious customs. This column was located in a Celtic-Ligurian sanctuary in southern France. It shows twelve carved human heads.

Right: A sacred site, surrounded by a ditch, inside which animal sacrifices were performed. The offerings were then thrown into ritual pits as offerings to the deity.

Left: A ritual chariot from the late Bronze Age, found in Austria. The female figure which rises above the group and the figures which accompany it are from Celtic mythology.

RELIGION OF THE CELTS

Ancient Beliefs

Celts shared various beliefs with more ancient peoples, and contemporary peoples, and their mythology was to influence people in later times. Their world was rich in sacred places. Since they lived in constant contact with nature in a landscape of woods, pastures, waters, and hills, they often chose special places where they could establish contact with the deities of nature. They had sacred stones, woods, and trees (such as the beech, the yew, and the oak) and worshipped the spirits of springs and rivers. Following ancient traditions, the Celtic Gauls believed that animals also expressed particular aspects of the deities in symbolic ways. They practised the cult of the deer, of the bull, of the horse, of the boar, and of the dog. The animal itself was not the object of worship. The Celts worshipped the deity through the animal.

Another very ancient cult, also found in other peoples all over the world, was that of the skull. Skulls were placed on the walls of sanctuaries, in ritual niches, or in houses.

The Druids and Their Doctrine

At the peak of these religious concepts, there was a vision of the world which was religious and philosophical at the same time and was defended and perpetuated by the druids. The word *druid* was probably derived from a term meaning "of great wisdom." The druids celebrated sacrifices. They were priests, wise men, and philosophers. They were also teachers. They taught their students all the necessary information the young men needed to become members of the tribe and skilled warriors. Some youths were trained to become druids themselves.

The druids were well known in ancient Europe for their culture, which included knowledge of medicine, astronomy, geography, and natural phenomena. Divination and predicting the future were part of their art. The image of life, as expressed in their doctrine, was that of a constant interplay between the earthly world and the divine world. They felt that the divine world was accessible to human beings, or at least to some of them. The Celts believed that it was possible to experience various forms of existence. For example, there were tales of druids who could temporarily turn into deer or other animals.

Another typical element of Druid doctrine was the immortality of the soul. Souls were believed to live on after the death of the body reincarnated into other bodies. The social position of the druids was extremely high

Left: A procession of druids. *Inset:* The Gundestrup cauldron.

Right: Bronze mask of a deity, third century B.C. The eyes were filled with enamel or glass, and the mask was mounted onto a pole.

Left: Stone head of a Celtic hero found in Czechoslovakia, second century B.C.

The Gundestrup Ritual Cauldron

Cauldrons were used in the performance of Celtic rituals. They were often beautifully ornate and decorated to symbolize abundance and immortality. They were placed within the sacred sites and filled with inebriating liquids or precious objects. The cauldron found at Gundestrup (Denmark) probably dates back to the first century B.C. The cauldron was not found in one piece. The decoration which covered it forms a continuous frieze filled with mythological scenes and images of gods. The cauldron has a diameter of 69 cm and is 43 cm high. The detail (*above*) shows a god, the lord of the animals, in a seated position, wearing deer antlers and surrounded by wild animals.

even kings and powerful warriors were subject to their authority. Druids handled all legal issues and were judges in public and private matters. People who opposed their decisions were considered criminal. The druids shared a close common bond. They believed that their knowledge derived from a unique centre point in the universe.

Gods and Temples

Unlike the deities of Greek and Roman religion, the Celtic gods did not have individual responsibilities for war, peace, or prosperity. On the contrary, they had more general characteristics; the entity constantly changed and manifested itself in various ways. Roman statesman Julius Caesar said that one of the gods worshipped by the Celts was similar to Mercury but had universal authority. Taranis was the principal name of a god who was similar to Jupiter and appeared to be the lord of the natural elements. There were other gods who had complex tasks and features. The Celtic religion was steeped in elaborate symbols.

Sacrificial acts were performed on various occasions—before a battle, in case of illness, during drought, or during danger. The whole tribe, guided by the druid, took part in the ritual. The victims of the sacrifice were mostly animals, rarely people. The sacrifices were performed at sacred sites, which were surrounded by ditches. The necessary elements for the performance of the rituals were placed within this magic zone. These elements included an altar and ritual pits in which the offerings were placed. It was believed that, through a hole in the ground, earthly objects could more easily reach the deities of the underworld.

69

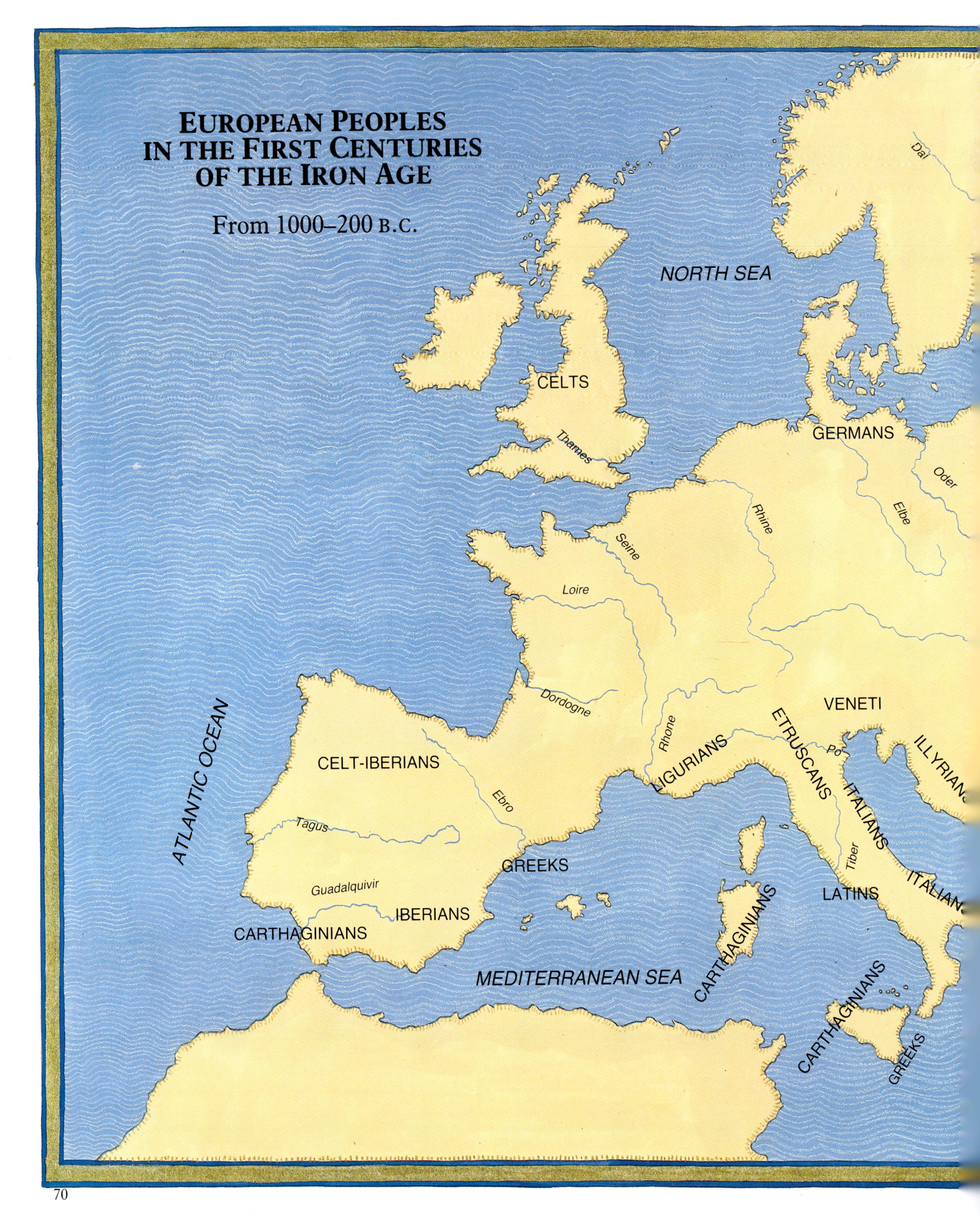

European Peoples in the First Centuries of the Iron Age

From 1000–200 B.C.

BALTIC SEA

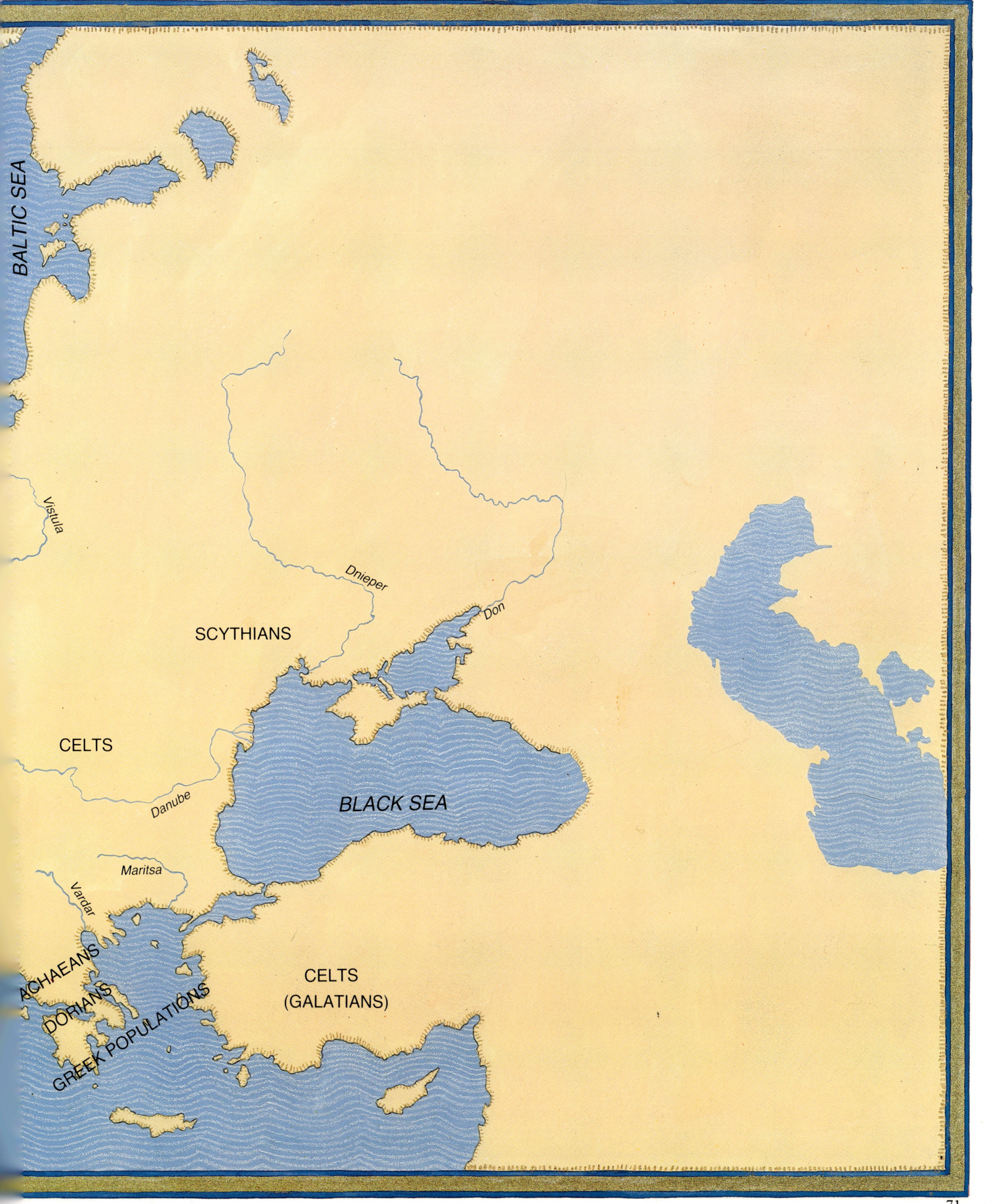

Vistula

Dnieper

Don

SCYTHIANS

CELTS

Danube

BLACK SEA

Maritsa

Vardar

ACHAEANS
DORIANS
GREEK POPULATIONS

CELTS
(GALATIANS)

GLOSSARY

abundant: more than enough; plentiful.

acculturation: to adapt to a new culture or environment; progressive assimilation.

agriculture: the processes and activities associated with farming; the work of planting seeds, producing crops, and raising animals.

anthropomorphic: having a human shape. Many of the stone deities from prehistoric times had anthropomorphic qualities.

archaeology: the science which studies the remains of human activities: everyday objects, tools, buildings, and artifacts.

archipelago: a group or collection of islands; a chain of islands.

artifact: any object made or crafted by human hands. Artifacts tell scientists much about early human cultures.

artisan: a skilled craftsperson.

astronomy: the study of the stars and planets.

Australopithecines: ancient, humanlike beings (hominids) which appear to be the closest relatives of modern humans.

barbarian: a primitive or uncivilized person (one who did not speak Greek).

barren: sterile; unable to reproduce or bear fruit.

camouflage: to hide or conceal by assuming a disguise or blending into the surrounding environment.

carcass: the body or remains of a dead animal.

catastrophe: a terrible or terrifying occurrence; a tragedy or disaster.

centaur: in Greek mythology, a fabled creature that is half man and half horse.

ceramics: objects made of clay that are moulded into shape and baked.

continent: one of the principal land masses of the earth. Africa, Antarctica, Asia, Europe, North America, South America, and Australia are regarded as continents.

corridor: a hallway or entrance space.

cromlech: a collection of large stone blocks (monoliths) arranged in some type of pattern to form a monument. The site of Stonehenge in England is an example of a cromlech.

cult: a specific type of religious worship, with its own particular rules and ceremonies.

cultivate: to prepare land for the planting and growing of crops.

currency: the medium of exchange, or money used, in any country or region.

deciduous: trees which shed their leaves each year during certain seasons.

dolmen: a prehistoric tomb or collective burial chamber formed by a stone slab set on top of two or more pillars.

domesticate: the process of taming wild animals and then using them for different purposes.

dugout: a type of boat or canoe made by hollowing out a log.

environment: the circumstances or conditions of a plant or animal's surroundings. The physical and social conditions of an organism's environment influence its growth and development.

epoch: the beginning of a new and important time period in history.

equestrian: pertaining to horses or to those who ride or perform on horses.

evolution: a gradual process in which something changes into a different and usually more complex or better form. Groups of organisms may change with the passage of time so that descendants differ physically from their ancestors.

excavate: to make a hole or cavity by digging; to form by hollowing out; to uncover or expose by digging.

fertile: rich in natural resources; able to produce and/or reproduce.

fossil: a remnant or trace of an organism of a past geologic age, such as a skeleton or leaf imprint, embedded in some part of the earth's crust. Scientists search for fossils to learn about past life.

glaciers: gigantic moving sheets of ice that covered great areas of the earth in an earlier time. Glaciers existed primarily in the Pleistocene period, one million years ago.

habitat: the areas or type of environment in which a person or other organism normally lives.

harpoon: a spearlike weapon with a barbed head used in hunting whales and large fish.

herbivore: an animal that eats plants. Elephants and deer are herbivores.

hide: the skin of an animal. Early humans made tools with sharp edges to cut animal skins to make clothes and tents.

hieroglyphic: a type of writing used mainly by ancient Egyptians in which certain signs and symbols were used to represent words instead of letters.

humid: containing a large amount of water or water vapour; damp. Warm air currents in coastal areas produce a humid climate.

hypothesis: a theory based on available supporting evidence.

immigrate: to move into a new region or country.

indelible: unable to be removed or erased; permanent.

ingot: a piece of metal, formed into the shape of a bar, used as currency in ancient times.

kiln: a furnace or oven for drying, burning, or baking something, such as bricks, grain, or pottery.

latifundia: during the Etruscan civilization, large stretches of land that were owned by a family group and farmed by slaves or peasants.

lethal: deadly; fatal; capable of causing death.

loess: a fine-grained, extremely fertile soil found widely in North America, Asia, and Europe.

mammoth: an extinct type of large, hairy elephant with curved tusks.

maritime: having to do with the sea or with the shipping industry.

megaliths: large stone monuments which can be found in different shapes and locations throughout the world.

menhir: a large stone block which can reach over 20 metres in height and is most often found standing on end in the ground, isolated. A menhir is a type of megalith.

mercenary: hired soldier; a soldier paid to fight battles in foreign countries.

microliths: little stone tools which were characteristic of Neolithic culture.

migrate: to move from place to place in search of food and shelter. Migration usually revolves around seasonal changes.

miniscule: very tiny; extremely small.

mollusc: any of a large group of animals having soft bodies enclosed in hard shells. Snails, oysters, and clams are molluscs.

monolith: something carved or formed from a single stone block.

moor: a large, open space of land which may be hilly or marshy.

nomad: a member of a tribe or people having no permanent home, but roaming about, usually with herds of grazing animals.

ochre: a natural red dye used extensively in the daily lives of ancient peoples.

oscillate: to move from side to side or back and forth in a regular pattern.

parched: dry; thirsty.

peninsula: a piece of land surrounded by water on all sides, except for a narrow strip which connects it to the mainland.

plateau: an elevated and more or less level expanse of land.

prey: an animal that is hunted and killed for food by another, stronger animal.

primitive: of or existing in the beginning or earliest times; ancient.

remote: distant; far away.

ritual: a ceremony or procedure, especially with regard to religious worship or magic.

sanctuary: a place of peace or safety; a haven or place of rest; a special building set aside for worship.

sarcophagus: a large tomb, usually heavily decorated or inscribed.

savanna: a treeless plain or grassland characterized by scattered trees, especially in tropical or subtropical regions having seasonal rains.

scimitar: a short, curved sword used by ancient warriors.

scythe: a long, curved blade set into a handle used to cut grass or grain.

simultaneous: happening or occurring at the same time.

situla: pail-shaped pot of bronze, decorated with scenes of everyday life.

sod: the top layer of earth, including grass and roots.

species: a specific type or class of plant or animal. Plant and animal species are usually very similar and can therefore interbreed only among themselves.

stele: a pillar or tall stone marker usually engraved with symbols or other inscriptions.

steppe: great grassy plains of central Asia, with few trees.

symbiosis: a coexistence between organisms which is advantageous to both.

temperate: a climate which is neither very cold nor very hot.

transhumance: the migratory movements and patterns of certain animals and the people who depend on them.

trilith: two vertical stone blocks topped by a horizontal stone block.

tundra: frozen plains of the Arctic.

urn: a large vase or receptacle.

valley: a space of low land wedged between hills or mountains that usually has a stream flowing through it.

venerate: to worship; to have great respect for.

INDEX

A

Acheans, 39
Achilles, 42
Aeneid, the, 52
Aeneus, legend of, 52
Agamemnon, (king), 42
agriculture (see farming)
Alexander the Great, 67
alloy, 22
Alps, 6
Alps, population of, 20-21
amber, 32-33
amber route, 33
animals
    domestication of, 16, 18
    in art, 15, 58, 59, 61, 64
    sacred, 37, 68
Apulians, 47
archaeological periods, 8, 10
Argonauts, 33
art
    cave, 13, 14-15
    Celtic, 65
    Etruscan, 51
    nature in, 65
    rock paintings, 14, 24-25
    Scythian, 61
Athena, 42
Australopithecus, 8

B

bifacials, 11
blacksmith, 23, 29, 50
Bosphorus Strait, 67
Bronze Age, 22-23, 30-31
bronze smelters, 29
Bruttii, 47
burial mounds, 35
burial rites, 15, 19, 27, 35, 38, 51, 56, 61

C

Camunians, 47
Carthaginians, 44, 46
Celtic civilization, 56, 62, 64-65, 66-67, 68-69
Celts, 46, 53, 62
    military techniques of, 66-67
ceramics, 19, 24-25
Chalcolithic Age, 29
city-states, Etruscan, 48

climates, of Europe, 6-7, 8-9
clothing, 14, 30-31, 60
colonization,
    Carthaginians, 46-47
    Celtic, 64, 66-67
    Etruscan, 56
    Greek, 56, 46-47
    Phoenicians, 46-47
Copper Age, 22-23
Corsicans, 46
cremation, 35, 40
Crete, civilization of, 36-37, 38
cromlech, 26-27
culture
    Indo-Europeans, 24-25
    Neolithic, 18-19
    transfer of, 22
curvilinear art, 65

D

dark centuries (of Greece), 40-41, 42
Darwin, Charles, 8
deities, 16-17, 25, 36, 42, 68-69
Diomedes, 42
Dionysius, (king), 66-67
divination, 51, 68
dolmen, 26-27
Druids, 68-69
dyes, use of, 15, 24
dynasties, 56

E

Etruscan civilization, 48-49, 50-51
Etruscans, 47, 52-53
Europe, ancient, 16
Evans, Arthur, 37
evolution of human life, 8

F

farming, 16-17, 18-19, 20-21, 30-31, 34, 41, 49
    origins of, 16-17
fire, use of, 9, 11, 14
fishing, 20-21
Forum Boarium, 52
fossils, 9
fratriat, 41
frieze, 42, 45, 69

G

Gauls, 46
genos, 41
geological epochs, 8
glaciation, 8-9
gods (see deities)
grave goods, 15, 38, 56, 64-65
Gravettian populations, 13
Greek civilization, 38-39, 40-41, 42
Günz, glacial period, 8

H

habitats, of Europe, 6-7
Hallstatt, 54
Hallstatt, population of, 56, 58-59, 62
Hector, 42
Hecuba, 42
Helen of Troy, 42
heroic ideal, 42, 59
hieroglyphics, 37
Hissarlik, 42
Holocene epoch, 9
Homer, 39, 42, 59
hominids, 8
Homo erectus, 8, 9, 13
Homo habilis, 8, 9
Homo sapiens, 8
Homo sapiens sapiens, 8, 13
horse, 32, 33
hunting, 10-11, 12-13, 20
hydraulic engineering, 49

I

Iberian civilization, 44
Iliad, the, 42
Indo-Europeans, 24-25
Industrial Revolution, 23
interglacial periods, 8-9
Iron Age, 23, 54-55
Italics, 46-47

J, K

jewellery, 29, 30-31, 51, 65
Julius Caesar, 69
Jupiter Capitolium, 52
Knossos, 36-37

L

La Tène, 62, 64-65
language, 24-25, 37, 51, 67
    dialects, 40-41

Latins, 47
Latinus, (king), 52
Lavinia, 52
Leptolithic, 12
Ligurians, 47
lintel, 26
livestock keeping (herding), 18-19, 41, 60
Lucanians, 47
Lyell, Charles, 8

M, N

malachite, 22
Mastarna (see Servius Tullius)
megalith, 26-27
Menelaus, (king), 42
menhir, 24, 26
menhirs, aligned, 26
Mercury, 69
Mesolithic period, 8, 10
metals, 22-23, 24, 29, 40-41, 50-51, 54-55
migration (of human populations), 29, 40
Mindel, glacial period, 8
Minoans, 33
monolith, 26-27
Mont Blanc, 6
moor, 7
moulds, casting, 29
mountains, 6
Mount Olympus, 42
Mycenaean civilization, 33, 38-39, 40
Neanderthal man, 8
Neolithic period, 8, 10, 17, 18-19
nomadic populations, 18, 46, 60
nuraghes, 34

O

obsidian, 32
Odysseus, 42
Odyssey, the, 42
oligarchic government, 48
origin, human life, 9

P

Paleolithic period, 8, 10
Paris, (Prince of Troy), 42
Patrocles, 42
Phoenicians, 44, 46
Picenes, 47
Pleistocene epoch, 8
Polyxina, 42
prehistory, 23
Priam, 42
priests, 26, 31

privileged classes, 34
Punic Wars, 46
Pylos, palace of, 38-39

R

raiding, 39, 66-67
red ochre, 15
religion, 20, 27, 34-35, 36-37
   of ancient Europe, 16
   of the Celts, 68
   of the Etruscans, 51
   of the Indo-Europeans, 24-25
religious symbols, 16-17, 24, 34-35, 51
Remus, 52
Rhaetians, 47
Riss, glacial period, 8, 11
Rome, 46, 52-53
   legend of, 52
Romulus, 52

S

sailing, 32-33, 50
salt, 54-55
Samnites, 47
Sardinians, 47
Schliemann, Heinrich, 37, 42
Scythians, 60-61
Sea People, 39
Servius Tullius, (king), 53
settlements, 21
seven hills (of Rome), 52, 53
Sicilians, 47
situlae, 58-59
smelting, 50, 54-55
society, organization of, 10-11, 30-31, 34, 41, 64-65
spear thrower, 12
spinning, 31
stele, 24, 66
steppe, 7, 60
Stone Age, 9
Stone Age, (New), (see Neolithic period)
Stone Age, (Old) (see Paleolithic period)
Stonehenge, 26
Strait of Gibraltar, 44
Styx, River, 42

T

taiga, 7
Taranis, 69
Tarquinius Priscus, (king), 53
Tarquinius Superbus, (king), 53
Tautavel, France, 11
temples,
   Celtic, 69
   Etruscan, 52
Terra Amata, France, 11
terra-cotta 30, 36, 47
thalos tombs, 39
tools, 10-11, 12-13, 14, 18-19, 22-23, 54-55
trade, 22, 34, 52, 56
transport, 22, 30, 32-33
trilith, 26
Trojan horse, 42
Trojan War, 42
tundra, 7

U, V

Ulysses, 33
Umbrians, 47
Veneti, 47, 58-59
villages, of the Neolithic period, 18-19
Virgil, 52

W

war, 34, 39, 59, 67
warriors, 38, 56, 67
weapons, 12, 22-23, 34, 54-55
weaving, 31
wheel, 22
writing, 36-37
Würm, glacial period, 8, 9

Z

Zeus, 42
zones, of vegetation, 7